"Leave it to Ragsdale and Saylor to combine reflection and critical thinking into fun activities for groups, classes, young and old! This book is a long-awaited treasure of reflective activities that promote analytical thinking and invite participants into a journey of self-discovery."

—Terry Silver, Associate Professor, The University of Tennessee at Martin, Educational Studies

"An outstanding resource for new youth leaders and teachers as well as veterans in the field! The reflection ideas and tips will help each learning opportunity meet goals and objectives. All the while, the group is having lots of fun."

—Dr. Nancy Dickson, Program Director, Humphrey Fellowship Program, Vanderbilt University

GREAT GROUP REFLECTIONS

GREAT GROUP REFLECTIONS

60 Compelling Challenges to Prompt Self-Discovery & Critical Thinking

Susan Ragsdale & Ann Saylor

powerful publications • energetic trainings

write creations group
Nashville, TN

Great Group Reflections: 60 Compelling Challenges to Prompt Self-Discovery & Critical Thinking
Copyright ©2019 by Susan Ragsdale and Ann Saylor.
All rights reserved.

Susan and Ann are available for giving book talks and also for leading games, professional workshops, and discussion forums via online or in person. Contact them at team@writecreationsgroup.com.

Published by Write Creations Group, LLC
www.writecreationsgroup.com

ISBN- 978-1-942743-99-6

Editors: Crys Zinkiewicz, Jackie Hansom
Cover Photo: Sunyu Kim, https://www.pexels.com/@mauveine
Yoga Poses: Linda Ragsdale
Cover Design: Susan H. Roddey
Interior Design: Susan H. Roddey

To Chip, Terry & Ellen
—the instigators of this particular rabbit trail of discovery—
thanks for asking the right question.

And, to our friends and colleagues
who think deeply, ask questions, and inspire people
to make the world a better place.

Don't search for the answers, which could not be given to you now, because you would not be able to live them. And the point is to live everything. Live the questions now. Perhaps then, someday far in the future, you will gradually, without even noticing it, live your way into the answer.

—RAINER MARIA RILKE

Contents

Activities

Contents

(cont'd.)

Getting Started

This book is about engaging others in reflective practice around group experiences and making the practice fun. One important role for teachers, afterschool workers, youth pastors, and mentors is to coach and guide young people as they make decisions. Projects, leadership roles, service experiences, and everyday choices all provide rich opportunities for reflection. In these various moments, adult guides can tease out teachable moments to help strengthen young people's capacity for critical thinking and growth.

Sometimes reflective conversations can stall out. Sometimes the questions simply generate a yes, no, or shrug-of-the-shoulders response. And those responses aren't limited to young people. Adults can be guilty as well of brushing off the practice of pausing to think more deeply or more broadly. It takes time to listen deeply and reflect.

Having some creative, engaging activities in your toolbox to pull your group into deeper contemplation is a must. Writing and journaling are the well-known tried-and-true methods. But, there is a plethora of ways to dive into reflection. Expanding how you frame reflection may just do the trick in engaging more members of your group. From movement-driven reflection to more artistic endeavors and beyond, imagine your group using yoga, nature, balloons, or even a round of Rock-Paper-Scissors as elements to stir deeper thinking.

Within these pages you'll find a variety of experiential reflection techniques. Each method is written up in the style of a recipe. For each process, you will see—

Activity Title

 Time—indicates the amount of time it takes to complete the activity from start to debrief (based on groups of 10–15 people)

 Supplies—describes any materials needed

 Prep—specifies any tasks best done beforehand

Directions—gives the steps to take for conducting the activity

Most activities require little-to-no prep, saving time in this on-the-go tool, useful for classrooms, athletic fields, or wherever you find yourself with youth or adult learners. Additionally, most supplies will be things you probably have on hand.

With some activities you will see an additional step to the process, designated as **Going Deeper. Going Deeper** questions are models for conversations that might evolve from the reflection activity. These queries are by no means limiting. You are free to ask whatever best fits what is happening in your group. We don't have seer abilities to let us know what will happen when your group engages in an activity or where you may need to steer the debriefing. We simply want to offer possible directions that guide the exchange from talking about the activity itself to a deeper dialogue about how or what they're learning and how they are increasing their awareness of others and/or the issue.

Whether you work with youth, adults or a mixture of each, we hope you'll be able to use these reflective practices to

- help participants deepen understanding of themselves, their team, and their world,
- develop 21st century skills such as initiative, leadership, communication, social skills, and particularly critical thinking and
- broaden perspectives of how choices and events impact others as well as themselves (i.e., empathy).

Additionally, as participants' insight and confidence grow, our hope is that they will more fully adopt a practice of examining the world, in which they'll realize the truth of Master Yoda's words, "Mind what you have learned. Save you it can."

Yes, with learning, with understanding, with compassion and with thoughtful action, we can change the world.

BE YODA, A MASTER GUIDE

Here are some guidelines to help smooth the pathway as we work with others in developing reflective practices:

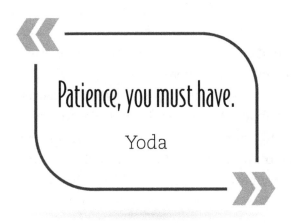

Patience, you must have.
Yoda

1. **No fixing. Be patient.** It's all about them. At times, we may need to be reminded that it's THEIR journey, and they need to learn and figure out things for themselves.

   Think about children who are learning to tie their shoes. It is easier, quicker and more efficient for Dad to tie the shoes, especially when he needs to be out the door and waiting on the child to do it will make him 10 minutes late. But, the child needs to learn how to do the task. Otherwise, Dad will be tying those shoes for a longer period of time than he needs to be! So, patiently, he takes the time to let his child tie both shoes.

   Working with others can lead to similar problematic moments. We know we can step in and do something or give the answer because we see it; we know it; we've experienced it. Impatience and the pursuit of efficiency, however, can backfire and let a moment slip by right when someone is prime to discover what they need to know. Be patient. Ask questions to help others learn from their own lives. Be patient with the pace.

2. **Stay curious. Ask questions. No assumptions.** I was at a restaurant with my four-year-old niece when she suddenly yelled out, "I HATE this restaurant." This was her first visit to this particular place. For whatever reason, I immediately assumed she didn't like the restaurant because of the food. But I resisted letting her strong statement close me off to curiosity. "Why don't you like this restaurant?" "Because," she said, "it's got so much W-O-O-D. I don't like that color." Assumptions are often our natural conclusions from logic or projections based on what we would think, feel or do in the situation. But our assumptions may not match the thoughts and feelings of the person experiencing the situation. Stay curious. Ask questions. Don't assume.

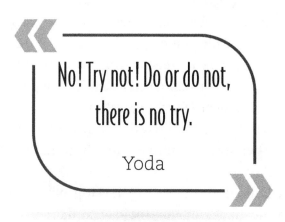

> No! Try not! Do or do not, there is no try.
>
> Yoda

3. **Make reflection time engaging.** Remember the sound clips of Charlie Brown and his teacher? The teacher's voice is indistinct noises that aren't being taken in by her class. (Wah wah wah wah wah.) For messages to have a chance of getting through and sticking with participants, learning needs to take place in an experiential setting. They benefit from different ways of interacting with the activity, content, or question. Crafting the space for self-discovery and aha moments requires us to pay attention to how we set the stage and conduct the experience.

For example, use brain-enriching activities suggested in our resource, *Brain Boosters in a Jar*®, which taps novelty, challenge, movement, music, and humor. Create moments for deep conversations. Use nature, visuals, group tasks, and individual time. Involve logic. Be mindful that people differ in how they process events and emotions. Add reflection activities that are invitational to both introverts and extroverts. Nurture their innate ways of processing and internalizing. There is no try. Only do. Vary your methods. Engage the participants.

4. **Make reflection routine.** Build the path. Ann, my longtime co-author, has 3–5 questions she asks her kids every day when they come home from school. What happened today that made you laugh? Where did you face and overcome a challenge? How did you make the day better for someone else? What is something you learned? What happened today that was good? The questions offer a springboard for conversation where Ann and her kids can both reflect upon their day and begin other conversations. Ann models her own commitment to reflection and growth.

As we build the path, we can develop our own set of thoughtful questions to ask during the day, at day's end, after an event, or after time spent with others. Try out your questions during or after service experiences, classroom lessons, projects, or weekend retreats. Personally, you can practice by reflecting with loved ones at day's end after work or school. You can also practice—and teach others to do the same—when facing conflict or making decisions. Again, simply think through the questions you need to address in these situations, then do the work of pause, reflect, then take action. As we teach group participants to reflect regularly, they will be more apt to adopt the discipline for themselves. This practice will help them for the rest of their lives.

Are you new to facilitating games or reflection time for groups? Do you have questions about how to pick which activities to use with your group? Do you need to refresh your memory of the basics so that you leave nothing to chance?

Check out our Tips for Game Leaders from *Great Group Games: 175 Boredom-Busting, Zero-Prep Team Builders for All Ages* on page 180. The question prompts will help you think through the nitty gritty details of your group and available resources as you plan out which activities or games will be the most relevant.

Why Ask Why?

Think of a field of study—such as religion, science, philosophy, research, education, technology, design, marketing, therapy, law, architecture, psychology, sociology, history, astronomy, and medicine. In almost every field, you are likely to find a common denominator. All ask questions. All seek something—be it understanding, solutions, improvement, information, expanded awareness, or empathy. Each field involves the art, discipline, and practice of questioning, reflection, and critical thinking. And a well-known tale teaches us why we don't have to look far to understand the importance of questioning.

LESSONS FROM THE BLIND MEN AND THE ELEPHANT

In the fable of the blind men who stumble upon an elephant, each man is making contact with a different part of the elephant. The men try to puzzle out what it is they have encountered. Each one describes the elephant to the others based on his personal experience: "This is a wall [elephant's side]," one says. The others disagree. "It's like a rope [tail]," declares another. "No, it's like a big hand fan [ear]" argues another. And so it continues. Each man is utterly convinced of his point of view, and only his point of view. After all, he's felt it; he's experienced it; he knows it.

This story reflects a habit we all easily and unconsciously fall into: thinking and believing that our viewpoint of reality is the reality. We sometimes presume we have the whole picture, believing everyone experiences things the same way we do. Our assumptions draw from our values, our personal history, and from our culture.

Truth, however, is very different. Take the story with the blind men. Each of their viewpoints stems from their own story of reality, from that moment they came in contact with the elephant. Imagine for a moment the difference if each man had made a different choice.

What if each man had asked questions, instead of assuming? What if they had tapped curiosity and reflection? What if they had shifted where they stood and "looked" at the elephant from a different place? If that had been the case, the men would have gotten new information and sensory input. They could have pieced together a more exact picture of the elephant, a more accurate interpretation of their shared reality. They would have gained greater understanding.

Then, there would have been a different moral to the story. Engaging in a practice of ask-answer-reflect-learn-ask again could have been a powerful demonstration in this revised imagining of the fable of how we can actively participate in our own evolution as individuals, a society and a culture.

This revised imagining of the fable could have emphasized how the consistent practice of reflection builds synapses in the brain and strengthens what is built through repetition. Fueled by practice, a pattern then begins to establish in the brain: curiosity, openness, questioning, reflecting, and critical thinking. When this pattern is reinforced and utilized frequently, it becomes embedded within the brain as a pattern of thought and problem-solving.

What if the men had demonstrated the power of questioning, reflecting, and critical thinking, then walked away determined to continue the practice they learned? Then, the moral of the story would have emphasized how we can use a deliberate method to become deeper thinkers and broaden our understanding of the world beyond our senses. Then the fable would have been entitled "The Wise Blind Men Who Named the Elephant."

Penny for Your Thoughts
THE INS AND OUTS OF REFLECTING

One of the activities we use to stress the importance of reflection after service experiences needs only one everyday item—a penny.

The task is simple. Without looking at a penny, everyone attempts to draw both the front and back of a penny. People then cluster into smaller groups and collectively determine whose drawing bears the closest resemblance to a real penny, still without looking at a penny.

Once each group makes their selection, the chosen artists hold their pictures out for everyone to see. Finally, each group looks at a real penny for comparison.

Then as a whole group, we focus our attention on what we can learn from this exercise.

- How were our memories similar?
- How did they differ?
- What aspects of a penny stood out for each person?

Then through reflection and questions, we tease out the parallel between the action we took in drawing a penny—and recognizing we had different memories—to our current circumstances: How is this experiment similar to... service work we do in the community/ our work on the group project/the weekend event? When we work together, do different things stand out to each of us? Do we all recall, verbatim, the same version of our shared experience?

No, we don't all recall the exact same thing. And that's the point.

Lessons from a Penny

Even though everyone will have seen a penny before this artistic task, elements will have been forgotten when it comes time to draw it. Different attributes will have stood out to different people (for whatever reason). Likewise, those individuals can participate in the same event and will all have different takeaways. For example, one person's takeaway may be an insightful conversation that led to greater understanding of the issue. Another person, upon reflection, may recall how inspiring it was to see someone with disabilities accomplish a task with ease and how seeing that changed the viewer's way of looking at the world.

Those nuances and kaleidoscope of impressions are the reason reflecting matters. The act of reflection lets a group capture what was important in each person's head and heart, thus enhancing the meaning of the experience as a whole, both for individuals and for the group. Additionally, reflection often leads to a greater sense of purpose for that group.

Reflection allows space to explore aha moments. "I never knew that was on a penny!" ("I never knew that was such an important part of what you're facing!")

It invites us to re-evaluate previous knowledge and to gain greater understanding. "Oh, he's looking to the left, but not the right, side of the penny." ("Oh! You really can't put plastic bags into recycling because they cause the machines to break down.")

Reflection can capture how we're shaped by our personal experience of culture, family, society, and values. Reflection also permits us to grapple with how our influences can seem similar and yet be so different. "Oh! I drew a 2016 penny, and you drew a 1999 penny. There's a similar base, but there are some distinct changes that were made to their features over the years." ("Wow! I always thought you and I believed the same thing about the environment. But now that we're talking about it more, I see how your experience is a little different from mine. So glad we had a chance to learn more about each other, as well as the environment!")

Two Sides of the Same Coin

The penny exercise also reminds us that we need both sides of a story. For example, our group needs to move beyond our perspective on situations or how we interpret an issue to thoughtfully consider the flip side as well. The other person's viewpoint is equally important. We need the perspective and understanding of the people who face the given issue on a daily basis. We especially need their way of looking at something when we don't know their circumstances intimately. Other people live with it, so they are impacted by it on an emotional and physical level.

Contrast that personal experience with the more intellectual perspective of a group of volunteers who have had no practical experience with the issue. Thus, both "sides" of the coin (viewpoints, understanding, and leadership) are needed to have a more complete understanding. The payoffs of this exchange include making a difference in the "giver" of service and in the "recipient" of service.

Thus, the penny exercise reminds us that we serve with not for. This idea is particularly true if we want to contribute to real change. Looking for ways to empathize rather than sympathize leads us to ask questions and to learn more about the experiences of those around us. We become better at soliciting and involving all voices to expand our impact.

Many of the above points can also be said of other areas in which we can engage in questioning and reflection. For example, what if you are negating conflict or are exploring career fields. These scenarios both benefit when time is taken to consider another's point of view and experience. Individuals grow when they seek to understand and to empathize. When they ask questions in this spirit, they take in new information and expand their mindset and capacity.

For instance, if participants are reflecting on a potential career path, they need to move beyond their limited understanding of the career field to learn from others who are doing that work. They need to talk with professionals in the field to hear what the day-to-day work looks like. They need to talk to various organizations to find out more about their work climate. They need to look at salary averages and get advice on how the career might impact financial decisions. Just as in the penny activity, they will discover there are numerous differing perspectives they will want to consider as they make their choices about work and life.

Thus, classroom activities, lesson plans, events, or leadership decisions all benefit from taking time to reflect and learn. The personal development benefits are tremendous when reflection is carried out intentionally. That intentionality is key.

THE BENEFITS OF REFLECTING

Reflection is a time to look back with careful consideration of what happened, what was accomplished, and what it all means. Reflection unearths new discoveries and learning. And yet, reflection is often the most neglected facet of any group experience. Frequently, it is left out altogether, often for the sake of time. To act without reflecting is to leave the occurrence incomplete, full of holes that can only be filled by those involved.

When we take the time to reflect, encouraging everyone to think critically and learn from their service, amazing transformations can take place. Intentional reflection creates deeper, longer-lasting positive outcomes for participants. It is a mirror that helps us to more truly see the world and ourselves as we really are. Consider these benefits. Reflection can—

1) **Solidify learning.** Reflection connects the experience to everyday life. It encourages higher-level thinking, as individuals look for root causes of complex problems, such as when students learn that algebra is important life skill, or when history students realize the significance of history's impact on current events.

2) **Encourage change in attitudes, beliefs, and values.** Reflection helps participants learn from both positive and negative experiences, guard against reinforcing inaccurate perceptions or biases, clarify values, and even begin new habits for healthier lifestyles.

3) **Set the stage.** Reflection prepares individuals for new learning and experiences yet to come.

4) **Further personal growth.** Reflection allows us to build self-confidence, develop skills, feel a sense of accomplishment, and develop critical thinking skills.

5) **Catalyze awareness.** Reflection encourages a broader perspective as participants engage with their peers and community around them. They get the chance to witness how daily experiences of life differ for everyone. They can begin to recognize how intertwined their well-being is with that of others.

The key is to be intentional! Let's say it again: The key is to be intentional! Reflection is very easy to skip over. Once you have a toolbox of reflection ideas (like this book in your hands), we hope you will feel SO comfortable and confident in engaging in reflection activities that allocating time for reflection is no longer an issue. It's of essence.

We are encouraged as a society to *do, do, do,* and to multitask so much that sometimes it's questionable whether or not what we "do" in all of our doing is done well or not! Rarely is time budgeted to process and discuss. We have too many demands to meet, too many curriculum and classroom objectives to accomplish. Often we are focused on trying to check everything off on our to do list. But grappling with complexities makes us stronger in mind (critical thinking) and spirit (empathy). Carve out the time and ask the hard questions—that's how you'll see the most powerful growth in your team.

Question Models

It starts with toddlers. We need look no further than those wobbly small ones in our everyday lives to realize that asking questions is part of our nature. We want to understand the world and connect with it in a meaningful way. And as the toddler stage indicates, we can be persistent in pursing that demand to figure out what's going on around us. Anyone who has been on the receiving end of a toddler uttering "Why?"—seemingly, or actually, after every sentence—can appreciate the tenacity of toddlers!

While at times frustrating, this quizzical stage is part of our natural development. Questions indicate an increasing awareness. Questions demonstrate an expansion of understanding taking place. At this stage, toddlers are reaching out beyond their sensory input (sights, smells, sound, tastes, and touch) and assigning values to ideas. The brain is starting to puzzle things out.

Inquisitiveness doesn't end when toddlers grow older. Rather, it is just the beginning—particularly if we cultivate curiosity. Some of the very people we deem wisest routinely use questioning and reflection to prompt continued learning, insight, and growth.

THE 5 WHYS MODEL

Sakichi Toyoda, inventor and founder of Toyota, created a process called the "5 Whys," in which people ask and answer five "why" questions. The goal is to answer each question with facts (no guessing or jumping to conclusions) until you find a concrete solution that can make a realistic change. Five is not a magic number; groups may ask fewer than five questions or more than five questions. It works best with issues that run from simple-to-moderately-difficult in nature instead of incredibly complex challenges.

The 5 Whys method is a tool for digging into cause-effect relationships, drilling down to discover root causes. Where could an action step be taken to counter the problem? How could it be prevented in the future? Here is a concrete example of the 5 Whys:

Problem: Female sea turtles are having trouble finding the quiet, dark beaches they need to nest. And if they nest anyway on a typical beach, their hatchlings are in danger of losing their lives.

Question: Why is it happening?
Answer: When female sea turtles come ashore to lay their eggs, their sense of direction is diminished. As a result, they may not nest at all. If they do nest, their hatchlings are also easily disoriented.

Question: Why is that happening?
Answer: Neither adult nor hatchling can orient to the horizon. Their confusion may cause them to move inland instead. And for the hatchlings, that can lead to dehydration, exhaustion and a greater susceptibility to predators.

Question: Why is that happening?
Answer: The artificial lights of businesses, hotels, condos, and other dwellings near the beach compete with the horizon's lights.

Question: Why is that happening?
Answer: An increase in coastal building intensifies indoor and outdoor lighting.

Solution: The simple solution is to change the type of lights used in developments, particularly during nesting season, so that they are 'turtle-friendly' (exchanging bright lights that emit white or short wavelengths for low-pressure sodium-vapor lighting [LPS], or using turtle-safe lighting: pure red filters or amber bulbs). Another easier-to-implement idea is to close opaque curtains or blinds after dark to mask windows facing the beach. Businesses and homes could also redirect their fixtures away from the beach, or even lower their height enough for dunes and vegetation to block their lights.

THE SOCRATIC METHOD

Socrates, the Greek philosopher and teacher, turned the asking of questions into an art. The Socratic method uses dialogue as the platform for provoking critical-thinking as well as drawing out both ideas and hidden presumptions. Probing questions—questions beyond yes or no—drive development and stimulate growth. In these conversations, answers can emerge that bring about change, both within individuals and within the world.

This method is helpful for practicing questioning and training people to use their brains to reflect first before speaking. This approach works well to explore complex issues or ideas and to open up societal issues and problems. The Socratic method uses open-ended questions and clarifying questions to probe assumptions, beliefs, reason and evidence. All voices are heard. Silence, too, can be part of the circle.

What if a group is exploring global warming? A conversation using the Socratic method might look something like this one:

Question: What is happening to our climate locally that you have noticed?
Answer: It's getting warmer.

Question: How do you know it's getting warmer? What's your evidence?

Answer: Icebergs are melting. Mountains in national parks are losing snow. Summer temperatures are lasting longer into fall. That's what the news says.

Question: Are you saying you've seen icebergs melting yourself? Are you saying you've learned global warming is happening from meteorologists? (Examples of clarifying questions.)

Answer: No, I haven't seen it myself. I have learned it's getting warmer from the news and from social media posts.

Question: Are you assuming newscasters and people on social media have proof that global warming is real?

Answer: Well, I think they've learned that fact from scientists.

Question: What proof do the scientists have? How do they know?

Answer: My dad is a scientist, and he taught me that scientists are able to measure the Earth's core temperature. He also talks a lot about the ozone layer. But I don't remember exactly how the ozone layer connects to climate.

And so the conversation continues as the group digs into what the temperature is now versus the time period scientists have been tracking the temperature. Using the prompt about the ozone layer, the group can focus next on what other factors might contribute to increased warmth. They can seek out evidence to support or negate the starting position. And, all the while, they can hypothesize and think through implications of actions, causes and effects, and how and why Earth's climate is changing.

One of our reviewers, Terry Silver, Associate Professor, The University of Tennessee at Martin, Educational Studies, provides sentence stems to help her group learn to frame their questions. She also uses anchor charts so students can hold the charts in their hands as they engage in discussion. These tools provide participants with guidance for how to stay open and curious in conversation and not digress into arguments. The stems help them ask questions and make statements that keep the conversation going with prompts such as—

I agree with_____because...

I sort of disagree with_____because...

Why do you think that?

Where can I find that in the book?

So, what you're saying is...

Couldn't it also be that...?

Can you explain what you mean?

Can you tell me more?

Can you give me an example of that?

THE WHAT? SO WHAT? NOW WHAT? MODEL

In agencies, K–12 schools, and universities, five little words easily frame many efforts to instill critical thinking in the reflection process: "What? So what? Now what?" This model introduces a logical progression of higher-level questioning. The progression helps the brain funnel information from broad to specific, from intangible to tangible, from past to future, and from general to personal. The model provides a natural flow of questions which are easy to remember in sequencing.

Asking "What?" gets at the tasks within and the facts surrounding the activity. Answers cover: What we did. Where we went. Who or where we helped. How we served. What we accomplished. What the results were. What academic/technical skills did each of us apply/use? What impact (addressing community needs) are we seeing or did we see?

Asking "So what?" leads us to a more thoughtful examination of our actions' meaning, both to us and to those we helped.

- Did the experience mean something to us personally?
- Are we changed in some way?
- Has our perspective altered?
- Has our understanding or knowledge been enhanced?
- Are our hearts different?
- Will we act or behave in some new way now as a result of this experience?
- Will we look at others with fresh eyes?
- What do we now understand about working with others verses working for others?
- Will things change for the better for the people or place we are leaving?
- Were there any negative consequences or outcomes?
- What did our presence and action mean to others?

Finally, the question "Now what?" leads us to thinking more about the future. What short-term and long-term impacts did we make? (If appropriate and you want to go deeper, ask specifically about the impact on the participants themselves and on others.)

- Is another action step begging to be taken?
- Is another strand of the root problem immediately obvious that needs addressing?
- Will tackling another root cause take us in a new direction and a new project?
- Or, do we want to dig in more to this problem to gain a deeper understanding?
- What will we do next, now that we know more?

The What? So What? Now What? method helps participants process their thoughts, feelings, and the potential implications of their actions. The phases, along with their potential questions, are outlined below as a direct conversation between a leader and their group:

What?
What happened? What did we do?

Answer: We helped a family in need.

Answer: We collected groceries for them because they're too busy going to the hospital.

Answer: And we made some meals they can put in the freezer and pull out when they need it.

So What?
What does our effort mean to you? To us? To the community? What did we learn?

Answer: The family was so thankful that we did what we did. It meant a lot to them.

Answer: I think our actions showed them that their community really cares.

Answer: I learned that small actions have a huge impact. Making a casserole didn't take a lot of time, but it sure seemed to take a lot of stress off of the family.

Answer: Our effort showed me that kindness is worth the time. It's a small price to pay when it can help so much.

Now What?
What are our takeaways? What's next for us? What do we do from here?

Answer: Serving made me realize that there are others who could benefit from our actions. What about other hospitals? Shut-ins? Nursing homes?

Answer: I want to know if there are organizations that do what we did.

Answer: I wonder if schools need the same kind of support we provided for this family today. Who in school might need help with meals or other essentials?

Answer: This project makes me think about kindness overall. What if we did something kind for those who don't normally get recognition, like the cafeteria or janitorial staff?

SAMPLE PROMPTS USING "WHAT? SO WHAT? NOW WHAT?" FOR A SERVICE-LEARNING EXPERIENCE

(Translation: Make the questions your own for other types of experiences!)

WHAT?

This phase taps into concrete thinking and asks about what happened. Participants describe the facts and events of the experience (who, what, when, where). They don't get into interpretations or judgments—just the facts.

- What happened? What did we do?
- What issue did we address?
- Who did we serve? What population?
- What were the results of our actions?
- What part was most challenging?
- What part was the most satisfying?

SO WHAT?

This prompt gets a little more personal. Questions help participants to discuss their feelings and ideas about experience as well as their analysis of the whole event.

Think about yourself:

· What feelings arose throughout the experience?
· What ideas popped up around the issue we set out to address?
· Did any new issues arise that we didn't anticipate?
· Were there any questions that bubbled up related to the issue? What were they?
· What are you learning about yourself through this experience?
· So what does this experience mean to you overall? What impact did this experience have on your values, your opinions, or your beliefs?
· Has anything changed for you as a result of this experience? If yes, what will you do, or how will you behave differently?

Think about our group:

· What are you learning about others in the group?
· How did the group work well together?
· Are there ways we could have accomplished our goal more effectively?
· Where could we have been more intentional along the way?
· How did we do in these areas: Showing compassion? Being respectful? Listening? Being open to learning more from those we worked with in the community and about the issue itself?

Think about the experience:

· What did you learn about the issue? About those we served?
· Did we work together with them or did we find ourselves trying to simply do for them?
· How did our actions address the issue?
· How did our actions impact the people involved?
· Where do we know we had a positive influence?
· Did we make it easier for people to claim their own power and voice? How?
· Did we address a pressing need? How or how not?

- Where, if anywhere, did we unintentionally contribute to the problem? Did we have assumptions we acted on that we discovered were wrong? Did we accidentally say something that was taken the wrong way?
- What can we learn from our own attitudes, words, and actions that will help us be even more affective in our next work? (This can be a place where you can address any observed negative stereotypes or unintentional harm that was caused.)

Now What?

This stage of the questioning progression moves your group's thinking toward real-life applications. Thinking here is more abstract. "Now what?" zooms out to look at the big picture surrounding the project and think about broad implications beyond impact on themselves. How might our service affect future decisions, studies, goals, priorities, and actions for us as individuals? As a group? Or, as a community?

- What are possible root causes of the problem we addressed?
- What other actions need to be taken to directly address the root causes?
- Who else did we learn of (agencies, individuals, laws) that might be working on this issue? Whom might we seek out to learn more from or work with next time to increase both our impact and theirs? Where can we ally?
- What can we do with what we learned today? How can we apply what we learned to advance our work on this issue or to apply our learning to another issue or situation?
- Are there any lingering questions we have about this issue that we'd like to have answered? What else do we want to know or learn about regarding this issue or population? (Recording answers on paper or a device is a good idea!)
- Where do our questions and passions need to take us next? In other words, now what will we do knowing what we know now?

Do we want to dive deeper into this issue continuing what we started? Do we want to stick with this issue and address another root cause? Or, do our concerns lead us elsewhere to serve next?

- Is there any follow-up needed from what we just did?
- And, how will we pass on what we learned to our peers and the community so that they, too, can learn from our experience?

TIP

When leading this model of reflection, be prepared to prompt the transition if needed between each phase saying something like, "Now, we'll move into talking about 'So what?'" then ask the questions desired. Keep the group focused on drawing out the connections between action, understanding and application to real life. Tangents may occur. Simply pull people back on point. Reiterate the main points (or skills learned) at the end of the discussion to sum up what was learned or achieved.

Wrapping Up the Questioning Methods of Reflection

Whatever the method choice, questioning is a fitting approach to deeply reflect upon what it takes to best determine where change is needed as well as what one learns while leading and implementing change. In the next section we'll explore different methods for leading reflection beyond a conversational model. But for now, we want to reiterate the importance of creating this thinking process as an essential habit for personal development, life, and even workplace skills.

Use of any of these three techniques will establish reflective patterns that become habit with repetition and serve individuals as well as groups. The key is to let ask-answer-reflect-learn-ask-again become a model of thought and habit.

Good questions stimulate critical thinking. Queries draw out ideas, and they can be used to analyze concepts. Questions dig into fundamental principles, concepts or theories to test what is valid, real and true.

Reflection can unearth unconsciously held beliefs. Continued questions challenge assumptions to get to truth and accuracy. Our empathy skills are developed. Our brain wiring for generosity and connection to others is strengthened as we seek to understand life experiences from different perspectives. When we embrace the reflection routine, we have better, more accurate information to make informed decisions. And, we are able to move to greater depths of wisdom and understanding.

We can turn reflective questioning into a habit. Simply practice the method: ask a question, then listen, reflect, and then ask another question. Repeat this course of action. Stay curious and continue to ask-answer-reflect-learn-ask again until the process becomes second nature.

The more one practices something—by doing, reading, learning, discussing, teaching—the more connections are made within the brain to "get" that topic or activity. Repetition, or practice, makes something permanent. Thus asking questions isn't simply about seeing if an individual understands a topic of study. Asking questions is about developing a disciplined practice of reflection to build critical thinking skills, openness and the ability to continue learning, examining and growing for all areas of life.

As this discipline evolves, a lifetime habit develops. And that habit can result in a more enriching life. The practice will encompass reflecting on each day's experiences, reviewing our work on the job, seeking new opportunities in our encounters with people and pursuing understanding about root causes of conflict and divisiveness—we can apply thoughtful probing to better ascertain how we want to respond in any given situation. We can become greater thinkers and students of life.

Strengthening Reflection

INTENTIONALLY TIMING YOUR REFLECTION

As you choose your reflection techniques, you'll also want to keep in mind the timing of your reflection. When will you reflect? Be intentional about where you want to take advantage of teachable moments: pre (project, event, lesson plan, service), during the experience and post (project, event, lesson plan, service) are all viable places to check in.

PRE-REFLECTION:

The preparation stage, before you commence, is a chance to pre-assess. Participants can explore what they think the experience, people, and project will be like. Taking note of what is said in this stage lets you compare to what is shared post-activity. This practice lets you see what has changed for the participants in your group. Pre-reflection is also an opportunity to clarify boundaries and expectations, explore fears, discomfort, anticipation and excitement. You will determine if the group is clear about what is expected, if they feel prepared, and if they are on the same page. You may also find out what ideas or impressions the group has about the community they will be serving.

DURING REFLECTION:

Mid-project reflection offers a chance to touch base in the muck of your work together. Groups often check-in regarding whether or not they are doing what they set out to do and assess if that is okay. They look at their frustrations and name what's going well. They identify if any adjustments need to be made with regards to either frustrations or capitalizing on strengths or previously unseen opportunities.

Post-Reflection:

Post-activity reflection offers closure to the emotional, spiritual, and physical experience of what the group underwent. Considering the whole process puts the icing on the cake as the group talks about what they learned from the experience. They evaluate if needs and goals were met, and they assess what they could do better next time. They think about next steps and what other actions they can take now with their new understanding, knowledge, and experience. And, they consider how they might view issues differently because of their involvement.

Reflect & Learn

Reflection can and SHOULD take many forms. Yes, the basis is asking questions, so that obviously indicates a conversation. However, that conversational reflection doesn't have to be done merely sitting in a circle with a predictable back and forth dialogue. Many people need space and time to think about what they know or are learning and can't simply blurt out answers—especially our introverts. And before we turn to the next usual suspect, journaling, let's just say that both of those are the easy ways to reflect. We want to vary our reflection by using other forms of engagement.

The use of a "third thing" (activity or prompt) provides just the right tool to allow the group the time they need to think through what they really want to say, or what really is going on for them internally.

What is a "third thing"? In this case, it is use of an outside prompt upon which participants can focus some of their attention allowing a safe space to open up in which they can more fully be mindful and aware.

A third thing involves introducing an element that allows participants to use their hands, their creativity, and even their bodies to reveal what they are learning. Acting, writing poetry, finding an object in nature, crafting a play dough sculpture, doing art, keeping balloons up in the air, or doing yoga are all examples of a "third" thing. Each of these mediums can be used as tools while pursuing questions and insights.

These different mediums take the pressure off for coming up with an answer right this moment. They take off the pressure of feeling like everyone is looking at you and waiting for you to speak. Varied practices also support different learning styles, honoring the unique ways in which each person learns best just as they are. The exercises in this section offer a variety of third-thing opportunities to add new techniques to your toolkit.

TIPS

When it comes time to debrief the activity, whenever possible, have the group physically gather in a circle. This eliminates barriers, creates an open space, and reduces sideline chatter.

Note that if a question in the Going Deeper debrief uses the term you, then it refers to individuals and what they think. Questions that are geared to the group as a whole use the term we or us. The change in pronouns indicate the transition of focus.

Finally, revisit the Be Yoda, A Master Guide tips covered on page 3 to keep yourself on your toes in creating an open, welcoming learning space.

Activities

1-2-3 Newbie Entrance

 5–10 minutes

 questions, chart paper, markers

Set the context for what your group will be talking about. Is it a field trip, a discussion topic, a community need, or something else? Ask the group the following 1–2–3 Newbie Entrance questions and chart their answers.

1. What is one impression you have about... (the community we'll be working with, the issue that we're addressing, the project we're doing, etc.)?

2. What are two questions you have about what we're going to do?

3. What are three facts you know about this topic?

Use their answers as a springboard for sharing information, correcting misinformation, establishing guidelines for behavior, and alleviating any concerns or questions.

After the experience, you can pull this pre-reflection out to compare what actually happened and what was newly learned to initial reactions and impressions to capture any changes.

This pre-reflection exercise pairs with 3–2–1 Exit, a post-reflection activity.

3-2-1 Newbie Exit

 5–10 minutes

 questions, chart paper, markers, charted answers from the 1-2-3 Newbie Entrance

Ask the following 3–2–1 Exit questions after the group experience. Let the group discuss their answers in smaller teams of 4–5 people, or lead them through the questions as a big group and chart their answers.

3. What are three things you learned from this experience?

2. What are two things you are still curious about or want to learn more?

1. What is one impression you have now that you didn't have before?

Use their answers as a springboard for comparing the post-experience to the pre-experience captured in notes during the 1–2–3 Newbie Entrance. Where did learning change or expand? What changes happened in their impressions of the issue? How do they feel now versus how they felt on the front end? What ideas do they have for next steps?

This post-reflection exercise is useful to compare differences in learning after leading the pre-reflection technique 1–2–3 Newbie Entrance.

Strengthening Reflection

Get Creative. Take advantage of what's on hand at your site. Use the supplies and the space that you have to reflect accordingly. For example, if you are doing a playground renovation project, consider conducting your reflection time on one of the structures. If your group loves to play freeze tag, let each member share a reflective thought when they are tagged. If you have been teaching an arts class to senior citizens, use those same materials to create a reflection collage or sculpture. If your group is studying Aztec culture, have them make a mural of their favorite traditions from that time period. Make it fun. Invite warmth and laughter.

Teaching Myself

 5–10 minutes

 paper, writing utensils

Ask the group to think about past challenges they successfully navigated. For example, when they were little, they learned how to tie their shoes. They learned the alphabet, how to tell time, how to make a bed, etc. Those were all new challenges at the time of learning, and they learned how to face those challenges to successfully accomplish the tasks.

When was the last time they had a problem and successfully worked through it? Have them record 1–3 problems they've faced and dealt with successfully. Give them 1–2 minutes.

Next, for each challenge/problem listed, have them think about: What were the tactics they used to gain success? What strengths, abilities, resources, or strategies did they tap? Give them 1–2 minutes to reflect and record ideas for strategies or tactics that came to mind that helped them.

Going Deeper

> » Invite the group to look at the places where they have already succeeded in their lives. What do these successes tell you?

- » If you look at all the tactics you've used in the past, do you see any themes to how you approach problem-solving?
- » Are there particular strengths, skills or abilities that seem to be of particular help?
- » What has been the biggest help to you in overcoming past challenges?
- » What attitudes also help you to persevere?
- » Are any of your past tactics relevant to how you can work through a challenge you are facing today?
- » How can you apply your past success tactics to our service work in the community to improve our chances of pulling off a successful project?

End by reminding the group that they HAVE overcome challenges in the past. That means they can and will do so again. There will always be challenges throughout life. However, the participants should know that they have the resiliency and power within them to succeed when overcoming obstacles, time and time again.

Change Agents

 5–10 minutes

 paper, writing utensils

Divide the group into smaller teams of 2-3. Distribute paper and writing utensils. Ask them to write vertically, one letter at a time, the phrase "CHANGE AGENTS." For each letter of this acrostic, they should think about a quality, value, skill or attitude they personally have that fits each letter. What do they bring to the table? How can they help create change? Why will the world be better after they've tackled an issue? Give them 5 minutes to work.

If using this activity as part of a classroom session, clarify that the word should directly relate to the lesson or activity the class just completed.

Then, instruct the teams to take 3 minutes to create a 30-second commercial to promote their Change Agent selves. When time is up, take turns having teams perform their creation.

> *This activity can be used before doing a service-learning, project-based learning or group project to assess the talents ands skills everyone in the group possesses. Or, it can be used after the project is completed. If used during post-reflection, remind the group, when giving instructions, to link their answers directly to the work they completed.*

Balloon Launch

 10–15 minutes

 6 inch balloons, painters tape, 4–6 soft rounded tip permanent markers

 Use tape to mark a starting line for the balloon launch.

Distribute one balloon per person and ask them to blow up and tie off their balloons. Ask them to take turns using the permanent markers to write on their balloon a future goal or dream they have for themselves as a change agent. What do they want to do help others? What difference do they hope to make?

When everyone is done, have them line up behind the starting line. On "go" everyone should launch their balloons (Tip: pull back on tab of the balloon to let it fly or tap the balloons to send them off). Then, everyone scrambles to pick up a balloon that is not their own. Gather the group back into a circle. Invite them to take turns reading aloud the dreams written on the balloons. Celebrate each one with finger snaps.

Going Deeper

» How can we encourage each other as we pursue our dreams?
» What do we need to do to realize some of our dreams as change agents?

Strengthening Reflection

During the Action Phase

Reflecting during the action phase is possible. Simply checking in with your crew as you move around or as one of the youth leaders supervises works well. Pull from the following options to assess where adjustments might need to be made for the team.

How's it going? What are you enjoying/not enjoying from this experience? Where are you excelling? Where are you not doing so well? (Their answers point toward their emotional reactions.)

What are you learning? Who are you learning from? Who stands out as someone who is helpful and supportive? Where do you want to get better at doing something? (Their responses capture the learning aspect.)

Is there anything you want to try differently in what you're doing? (Their ideas point toward their thinking things through and to possible choices for behavioral change.)

Where have your current efforts, choices and work led you? (Their assessments point toward results.)

Balloon Notes

 10–15 minutes

 writing utensils, scrap paper, 6 inch balloons, painters tape, 4–6 soft rounded tip permanent markers

 Use tape to mark a starting and finish line.

Distribute a writing utensil, paper, and balloon to each participant. Ask them to write down one goal (for pre-reflection) or takeaway from the group experience (for post-reflection) on their paper, then roll up the paper. Next, instruct them to slip their paper inside of the balloon, blow up the balloons, and then tie off the balloons.

When everyone is done, divide the group into smaller teams of 4–5. Designate where each team will line up on the starting line. Have members place their balloons behind the finish line directly across from their starting point. On "go" the first person in each line runs to the finish line and grabs a balloon from their pile. They pop the balloon, grab the written reflection, and run back to their group. Once there, they read the reflection aloud, then the next participant goes. Repeat process until everyone has finished.

Have each team share one reflection aloud within the big group.

Peaks & Valleys Reflection

 15–20 minutes

 paper, writing utensils

Explain that you want the group to reflect on the service experience in its entirety. Ask them to draw a line graph, labeling both the peaks— high points/successes /growth spots—as well as the low points— challenges/obstacles/frustrations. Give them 5–10 minutes to work. Then use their work to discuss emotions, what was learned and the impact that was made.

Going Deeper

» What is a high point we want to replicate next time? How can we bring that about?

» What skills/strategies can we tap to deal with valley lows more effectively? What can we do differently or change in our approach to the lows?

» What did we learn from the valleys?

Coffee Measures

 15–20 minutes

 an assortment of variously colored and designed coffee mugs* (more than the number of participants in the group), water or some beverage

*Consider Goodwill or yard sales to find enough cheap coffee mugs.

Place all the coffee mugs on a table with something to drink as well. Ask everyone to grab a coffee mug that appeals to them—even if they don't want to get something to drink. Once everyone is seated, explain that participants will introduce themselves based on their mug choice and how it represents either who they are or how they like to lead others. For example, perhaps Rebecca chose a mug that had bold stripes in many different colors. She might introduce herself as a woman who has a bold personality with the courage to make tough decisions that make the world a brighter place.

Going Deeper

- » How well did your choice represent some aspect of who you are?
- » If you didn't get a mug you liked, which one does represent you best and what does it say about who you are?

Group Selfie Snap

 10–20 minutes

 questions, phone cameras—1 per group

Divide into small teams of 2–4. Give each team a copy of the questions set you're using (pre-reflection or post-reflection). Explain that each team will use their bodies to pose for pictures creating a snapshot of time. Each group must plan a pose in response to their question and take Selfie snapshots of the pose. They have 5–8 minutes to complete the task. When time is up, individual teams will take turns sharing their pictures. At least one person from each group should articulate what the bigger group is looking at as they show their pictures.

Question Options

For pre-reflection:

Option 1 (for groups just getting to know each other): Think about the best group project you've ever had or the best service-learning experience you've ever done. Share by snapshots what they were doing, why they remember it being great, what they enjoyed the most, and the most valuable learning from it.

Option 2 (for a closer focus on service-learning): Think about potential community issues that could evolve into a service-learning project. Create snapshots to indicate possible issues and what could be done to address them.

For post-reflection:

Option 1: Think about and have at least one photo pose to share for each question: 1) what happened, 2) what they enjoyed, 3) what was challenging, 4) an "aha" moment or something that stood out, 5) what they would doing differently if they had to do it all over again.

Option 2: Think about both the What? and So what? aspects of the questioning model . Craft selfie poses in answer to one or both of these questions.

Remember to take pictures of your poses! Returning again to the photos taken is a great way to reflect one more time as you celebrate.

The Powerful Poses

 15–20 minutes

 space

 If needed, review pictures or search online for videos on how to do these traditional yoga poses (pictured on next page). Make sure you keep the group safe as they do the different poses. Give participants a heads-up to wear pants and comfortable clothing on day of the activity (no skirts/dresses).

Have the group take in several deep breaths to quiet themselves down. Demonstrate each position in front of the group so all know how to perform the pose. Quietly, call out and assume the first position. Have them hold that position, breathing in and out, as they think about their answers to the question you pose. Allow 20–30 seconds before going to the next pose and question. Continue this flow of position, breathing, asking, thinking and moving on throughout the first circuit. Repeat circuit as many times as desired with new questions.

Mountain

Warrior 1

Warrior 2

Rag Doll

Extended Triangle

Balancing Stick

Hero

After going through the poses, sit down and ask if anyone wants to share anything that came to mind. Review each pose and the questions asked during that pose to prompt recollections.

- **Rag doll.** Where did you let go of something: a preconceived idea, an expectation, doing something your way, etc.?
- **Warrior pose.** Where were you brave?
- **Extended triangle.** This experience involved you, our group and those connected to the issue. Where did you deliberately work to connect with all 3 angles? What did you learn?
- **Balancing stick.** How did you balance helping out and also empowering others to do the same?
- **Mountain pose.** How did you maintain a positive attitude?
- **Rag doll.** Where were you able to relax in the experience?
- **Warrior pose.** Where did you stretch yourself to try something or do something new?
- **Extended triangle.** How did you connect with others in the group?
- **Balancing stick.** Was your view of the issue prior to working with it a balanced one or do you now have more information and understanding to create a better-balanced perspective? What has changed?
- **Mountain pose.** How did you maintain an open heart, stay ready to listen, learn and extend compassion?
- **Rag doll.** Where did you surrender and simply stay in the moment to experience whatever it had to teach?
- **Warrior pose.** Where were you brave and readjusted your perspective to try to see something from another person's point of view?
- **Extended triangle.** How did you connect with those involved with the issue? What did you learn from them?
- **Balancing stick.** Having experienced an issue, we realize that there are many things to consider to see the full picture. How

can you assess the many sources of information to get at the truth of a matter? How can you sort through all the information you took in to get a balanced understanding, one that may help unite and solve issues?

- **Hero pose.** Was there a moment where someone "saved the day" and was a hero? What was it? How can you be a hero every day?
- **Hero pose.** How can you use your powers for good? How can you use your powers to speak up for others, work for justice and spread kindness?

Strengthening Reflection

Let Goals Direct the Reflection

Process: If there are particular points you want your group to consider, make sure you have them in mind ahead of time. Then, you can throw into the mix of questions you ask specific ones related to your key points. Intentionally tie reflection into your learning objectives and service goals.

Potluck Recipes

 10–15 minutes

 paper, pencils

Divide the group into smaller teams of 3–5. Explain that teams have 8 minutes to create a recipe for a good _____ experience. (You fill in the blank with group, volunteer, project, leadership, or whatever you wish.) Their recipe should include the group, the problem or topic being addressed, and those the group will be working with (population served, community members, time period being studied, book characters, etc.). What ingredients and steps are needed to create a good experience and a significant impact?

For example, if a recipe were crafted for Social Justice, (the topic/problem) it might—

- Start with a base of understanding and reverence for all
- Add 1 heaping tablespoon of compassion and 2 tablespoons of listening
- Mix in 1 cup of respect
- Blend together until all ingredients are mixed well.
- Serve with action and advocacy for those who can't speak for themselves. Share with all. This starter kit continues to grow and expand when fed, resulting in a kinder neighborhood around the school.

After groups create their recipes, have each one share (or act out if there is time). Let the group ask questions after each presentation. Note any overarching themes or values that emerge across the various recipes.

This activity has multiple uses. Potluck Recipes works well to strengthen lesson plans where service or civic engagement is introduced for the first time. The recipes can be posted in a prominent place to remind the group of the behaviors, attitudes, and actions they want to emphasize while working together. The recipes can also be read aloud before a social studies or elections unit. Elements can be used to remind one another humorously of things like "splash it with compassion" while working on a group project. Finally, the recipes work well for groups to demonstrate knowledge after completing a project as, participants share their core "recipe," then reflect on how well their project turned out.

You can also make this a post-reflection-only activity. Having gone through the activity, what do they now know are key ingredients for impacting whatever topic was explored? What would they change in their recipe?

Tools of the Trade

 10–15 minutes

 chart paper, marker, paper, pencils, optional: actual, random appropriate tools of the trade, such as kitchen gadgets

Ask the whole group to name 6 or 7 gadgets or tools they might find in... (a kitchen, auto shop, cosmetology shop, carpenter's shop, etc.). List on chart paper. Or, if you bring gadgets in, have them select ones they want to use.

Next, divide the group into pairs or groups of 3, and then share one of these starter statements or one of your own (written out for the group to see):

- Writing poetry is like...because...
- Making a difference is like...because...
- Introducing a legislative bill is like...because...

Instruct groups to pick a gadget and finish the analogy. For example, if kitchen gadgets are being used, the analogy might be:

- Making a difference is like a blender because it takes everyone working together and sharing what they know and how they experience the problem being addressed to get the best results.

- Addressing climate change is like a strainer because there are so many misunderstandings that have to be separated from the facts before we can even make a difference.

Give them 5 minutes to work, then have all the teams share their analogies. Discuss as needed any key points or themes that arise, or ask questions to clarify.

The Analogy Is...

 10–15 minutes

 chart paper, marker, paper, writing utensils

Ask the whole group to name 6 or 7 items to fit the category of your choice. You can also ask participants to brainstorm the categories they want to work with after sharing a couple of examples to stimulate thinking.

Sample Categories
- Harry Potter Houses
- Divergent Factions
- Movie Genres
- Book Genres
- Amusement Park Rides
- Video Games
- T.V. Shows or Reality T.V. (name various shows that are relatable to the group)
- Game Shows
- Outdoor Adventures

List the called categories on chart paper. Then, divide the group into pairs or groups of 3. Share the starter statement (from below or one of your own written out for the group to see) such as:

- Putting together the school newspaper is like... because...
- Starting a new class is like... because...
- Visiting the Aquarium is like... because...
- Today the service experience was like... because...

Instruct teams to pick a category from the brainstormed list and finish the analogy. For example:

The Voice: Today working with our student council was like being on The Voice because I got to use my talents to shine, and I was in sync with the band (i.e. other student council members and the administration). Everything worked so well and smoothly. Even the judges (i.e. the principal and our advisor) gave me great feedback.

Outdoor Adventures: Putting together the school newspaper is like bungee cord jumping because there are so many ups and downs. You think you're getting the hang of what to do and bam! a sudden jerk of expectations or challenges makes you realize you don't know as much as you thought you did.

Give teams 5 minutes to work, then have all the teams share their analogies. Discuss as needed any key points or themes that arise, or ask questions to clarify.

My Kryptonite

 15–20 minutes

 Kryptonite questions list and a tossable object to be used as a "hot potato"

Have the group stand in a circle. Ask the group if they know what kryptonite is. (Superman's Achilles heel. It makes him vulnerable; it limits his strength and personal power.) Hand the "kryptonite" (a tossable object) to someone in the group and instruct them to start gently tossing the kryptonite around. Participants will pass it until a signal is used to stop the group (music, whistle blow or simply yelling "stop!"). Whoever is holding the "kryptonite" when the signal sounds must answer a question from the list about their own personal kryptonite, those moments that might keep them from being or doing their best while working with others. If tying to a specific lesson plan, personalize the questions to the activity or lesson being taught.

Option for multiple groups going at the same time: After the first person answers, they are now "out" and become the signaler for their group. They give the new question.

Kryptonite Questions

- The skill that will be most challenging for me in this group project is...
- An attitude I'll need to keep curbed...
- The hardest thing for me to overcome in working on this particular project will be...
- The struggle I think I'll have is...
- The thing I'm most worried about with this project is...
- When it comes to working with others, I have the most trouble with...
- When it comes to doing things I think are boring or uninteresting, I tend to...
- When it comes to doing independent work, I have the most trouble with...
- When it comes to talking with adults, I have the most trouble with...

Explain that Superman knew that Kryptonite was dangerous for him. He knew if he encountered it, he would need help. If HE needs help, it's okay for us to need help and ask for it.

Going Deeper

- » What makes you likely to not ask for help?
- » How can you overcome that obstacle and not let it hold you back from growing as a leader during our work together?
- » How can we support one another during this time?
- » How can we encourage one another to speak, act and respond in positive ways to challenges we'll face?
- » Batman is a different kind of superhero. He is known for using his brain. He does his research and looks at things from different angles. How can you apply Batman strategic thinking

and look at any challenges you encounter from all angles to come up with a new way to respond when things are hard or taxing? How does Batman thinking help in understanding the topic/community/issue we're exploring?

Adaption

Write numbers in various spots on a big beach ball. Have participants toss the "kryptonite" to each other. Each one shares the number nearest their right thumb when they catch the kryptonite. The leader reads the question corresponding to that number for them to answer.

Hero Perspective

 15–20 minutes

 chairs or painter's tape

Gather participants in a circle. Ask for one volunteer to stand in the middle without a chair. All other participants should sit in chairs (or put marks of painter's tape on the floor in a circle to mark spots on which participants stand with the volunteer standing in the blank middle space).

Assign each player a number (1, 2, 3) including the player standing in the middle of the circle. Everyone who is a 1 will be Hulk for the game. Everyone who is a 2 will be Captain Marvel. Everyone who is number 3 will be He-Man. Create together or go over the action/phrase for each character as described here:

Hulk: Hammers one fist into the palm of the other hand and says, "Hulk smash!"

Captain Marvel: Whispers "SHAZAM!" and then throws both arms above their head, makes fists and open and closes hands (jazz hands) to simulate lightning.

He-Man: Unsheathes his pretend sword, raises it above his head and proclaims, "I have the power!"

The volunteer in the middle should call out one of the three characters, Hulk, Captain Marvel, or He-Man. All the players representing the character called quickly jump up and move to another seat (or space) in the circle. However, there are two rules before moving. First, they must do the character action and say the hero cry. Second, they cannot move to the chair immediately adjacent to where they currently are. The volunteer in the middle tries to steal one of the empty chairs. Whoever is left without a chair becomes the new leader and must answer one of the questions listed for their character before they can call out the next character for the seat scramble.

Final rule. The volunteer in the middle can also call out "Avengers Assemble." When "Avengers Assemble" is called, all players must move to find a new seat. Again, whoever is left in the middle must answer a question from the Avengers Assemble questions.

The questions here work well with service-learning experiences. Simple tweaks in the questions easily transform it into a project-based learning activity reflection. For content connections, consider changing Hero Perspectives to Book Hero Perspectives, for example, with 3–4 characters from a book or play being read. Historical Perspectives could use Presidents and mottos to answer questions (Washington, "I cannot tell a lie…X was something I didn't like about this lesson.")

Character-Based Questions

Hulk "Hulk Smash!" (alternative: The Thing "It's clobbering time!")
- What preconceived idea changed (was smashed) as a result of this experience?

- What breakthrough did you have regarding your understanding of the issue?
- What breakthrough did you have regarding the population you served? How did your view change?
- What do you think it will take to smash through the problem and eliminate it altogether?
- What ideas do you have for how you can help break down this problem even further?
- If you kept one small piece of what happened today, what would you want to keep?

Captain Marvel "Shazam!"
- What values did you call on to be part of the experience?
- What insight hit you and changed your perspective on something during this experience?
- What new knowledge did you gain as a result of this experience?
- What skills did you use and strengthen? (communication, being open, using a hammer, etc.)
- What attitude do you now have about tackling issues and using your actions and voice to make a difference?
- What will you do next to make the community stronger and healthier?

He-Man "I have the power!"
- How did you tap your own power and use it for good? What did you do?
- Where did you see other people stepping up to use their power for good?
- Describe a moment when you felt powerful and able to make a difference. What contributed to that confidence and moment?
- What values did you act out as part of your own personal power?
- What did you learn about personal power from this experience?

- How can you be a superhero and make someone's day beyond when we're all together?

Avengers "Avengers Assemble!"
- When you arrived, what was your first thought about how the group would work together?
- How did the group communicate well?
- When and where did the group rally and work well together as a team?
- What skills did the group use and how did that help?
- What will the impact made today mean to each of you?
- How can you build off of this experience? What will you apply?
- What have you learned from this experience? How can that help to increase your impact next time?

Fun trivia (just in case someone in the group
wants to stump you): What does SHAZAM
stand for?

Solomon…Wisdom
Hercules…Strength
Atlas…Stamina
Zeus…Power
Achilles…Courage
Mercury…Speed

Strengthening Reflection

Build Skills and Make Life Applications to—

Process the Negative: Reflection is a perfect opportunity to process any negative feelings from the service-learning experience, including conflicts, fears and struggles. Resist dwelling on and consequently multiplying the negative. Focus rather on the opportunities that a challenging time provides to learn more about the issue, organizations, the community and ourselves. In tough moments, we can model reframing as well as praise participants for taking risks, doing a task well, maintaining a positive attitude anyway, or courageously stepping out of comfort zones. Building on healthy attitudes and decisions will reinforce these behaviors in future endeavors.

Build on the Positive: Honor everyone's voice. Look for what each did well, attempted or accomplished. Each team member should be a part of your reflection activities. During the event, be sure you look to catch each one doing good so you can name their use of strengths, skills, attitudes, helpfulness and positivity in action.

Hero Choices Toss

 10–20 minutes

 beach ball, markers, questions

 On a beach ball, randomly write down each of these hero names: The Human Torch, Green Lantern, Spiderman, Thor, Teen Titans, The Lone Ranger, The Shadow, Luke Cage, Wonder Woman, Thing, Underdog, Mighty Mouse

---

Gather the group in a standing circle. Designate someone to start. Explain they are going to toss the ball around. Whoever catches the ball looks at the hero name nearest their right thumb and calls out the name of the hero. The game leader reads aloud that hero's mantra and one of the questions corresponding to that superhero. (Questions are after instructions.) The ball is tossed again and play continues.

If all questions have been answered for a particular hero, have whoever has the ball look at the hero nearest their left thumb to get a new hero and new question.

The Human Torch: "Flame on"
- Who did you see "on," really going at it and working hard today?
- Who was a bright light?
- Describe a moment when you felt you were working in your full power of self.

Green Lantern: "In brightest day, in blackest night, no evil shall escape my sight. Let those who worship evil's might, beware my power—Green Lantern's light!"

- What light did we cast today? Did we diminish the size of a problem? How?
- What other issues need our light? Where do we need to do some work?
- How can we be a light for others?

Spiderman: "With great power comes great responsibility."

- When and why did your spidey-senses tingle today? (Moments when you knew you needed to pay attention, listen, or act)
- When and why did your spidey-senses tingle today around someone else? (Moments when you may have seen you needed to help someone else so they wouldn't feel uncomfortable)
- What responsibility do you now have regarding what you've learned? What work/action/advocacy is yours to do? Or, how can you go forward, knowing what you now know, and behave or choose differently?

Thor: "I say thee nay!"

- What is something in your life you need to say no to? Where do you need to work on setting healthy boundaries?
- What problem do we say nay (no more) to?
- What issue in the whole world is most important to you that you want to see eliminated (say nay!)?

Teen Titans: "Teen Titans, go!"

- To what problem is our group going to rally? Where do we need to focus our efforts?
- Name something we've done well together.
- Where do we want to go next?

The Lone Ranger: "Hi ho, Silver, away!"
- What is an action you and a friend can take to impact this issue?
- Why do you think it's important for individuals to use their power and take action?
- What is one problem you personally want to address?

The Shadow: "The Shadow knows."
- What do you know about ____(fill in the blank: this topic, this conflict, etc.)? How have you come by your knowledge?
- How can you share what you now know with others?
- What do you know is a skill or power you have that you can use in our work?

Luke Cage: "Sweet Christmas!"
- What will make this experience sweet?
- What was a moment during our experience that stood out to you?
- What strengthened your belief that actions can make a difference?

Wonder Woman: "Govern yourself with love, kindness, and service to others."
- How can you show love and kindness to others during our work together?
- How will you serve?
- What do you need to work on personally to live out Wonder Woman's mantra?

Thing: "What a revolting development!"
- What challenged you?
- How can we change things for the better?
- How can we keep a positive attitude even in the midst of "revolting developments" or situations that don't go as we hope?

Underdog: "Never fear, Underdog is here!"

- Do you think your simply being "here" made a difference? Why or why not?
- What is a way you can be "here" to others every day?
- Like Underdog, what is one thing we can always count on you for as we work together?

Mighty Mouse: "Here I come to save the day!"

- How do superheroes save the day? How do super humans save the day?
- What is a superpower you have?
- How do you "save" your own day? What helps you stay centered, caring and positive?

Going Deeper

- » Which superhero catch phrase motivates you the most?
- » Which superhero can you identify with the most?
- » What is your superhero service power?

A-Z Round Robin

 5–10 minutes

 none

Have the group sit in a circle. Going around the circle, one at a time, each participant speaks about an aspect of the group experience, lesson, or project that starts with the letter of the alphabet that hits them on their turn. The first participant will state an aspect that starts with the letter A. "Attitude was an important part of what we did." The next participant shares using the letter B. "Basketballs were a necessary tool for involving the kids." And, so it continues.

Participants have a 5-second count to start their answer. If they cannot think of something in time, they move to the end and the next person takes on the letter in question. Continue around the circle until everyone has spoken at least once, or go for the whole alphabet! (Can the group come up with something for letters like Q and Z? Feel free to skip harder letters if need be. But. It's a challenge to vocabulary and creativity. You decide.)

> By asking them to consider the important aspect of this group experience beforehand, this activity becomes be a pre-reflection tool. Consider other tweaks to make the question fit a pre-assessment of knowledge relating to a lesson plan or activity as well.

Road Signs

 12–15 minutes

 paper, pencils

Have participants use road signs to reflect on the group experience. They should draw signs and list out answers to their own map of the journey. Allow 5–8 minutes for crafting road signs.

Here are some possible signs you might use depending on what happened in your experience:

- **Detours**—adjustments during the experience, planning, or action phases
- **Green lights**—values, people, beliefs, or positive influences that were present during the experience
- **Yellow lights/Yield signs**—perspective, things said, something that happened, or new information they want to pause and think more about
- **U-turns**—changes in their own perceptions, perspectives, or thinking
- **Speed bumps**—challenge during the experience
- **Free parking**—an unexpected moment of joy or happiness

After everyone is done drawing, have participants pair up to share their images and some of what they thought about as part of their reflection.

Adapt connections to make this a pre-reflection event such as:

- **Green lights**—passions, knowledge, and skills I bring to the table that I'm excited about
- **Yellow lights**—things I'm cautious about in working with this issue/population
- **Speed bumps**—potential hurtles to pulling off the experience
- **Free parking**—what I'm looking forward to seeing happen
- **Detours**—our back up plan for when things go wrong
- **U-turns**—my ability to adjust on the spot is…

Have participants pair up with 1–2 other people to share insights from their maps.

Going Deeper

» What have you learned about yourself through this process?
» What road signs did you learn the most from?
» What have you learned about working with others to make a difference?
» If you were to reroute and repeat this road trip, which road signs would you want to pay attention to next time?
» What is something you've learned that will help you in the future?

Sentence Reflection

 10–15 minutes

 paper, pencils

Ask the group a question, such as, "What have you learned about yourself because of your involvement with the group and this experience?" Have participants write down a one-word answer in all capital letters running down the left-hand side of their paper. They then pass their papers to the left. Choosing one letter from their paper as their start to a sentence, the recipients express their feelings about the reflection question using that letter to kickoff the sentence. Continue passing papers until all words have been filled in with sentence reflections by different people. Return the papers to the original-word scribes, and ask for volunteers to share an answer that stands out from their papers.

Show Time!

 15 minutes

 internet access and an electronic device for each team (optional)

Divide the group into smaller teams of 2–4. Ask them to choose a song that expresses something their team hopes will happen as a result of their work, that they want to remember from their tine together, or that they experienced while working together. Remind them, if needed, to keep the song G-rated. For added fun, let teams use a social media channel to find their song and play a clip for the larger group. Allow 3–4 minutes for teams to pick their song. Then, teams take turns sharing key lyrics from the songs and explaining their song choice.

Going Deeper
>> What themes did we see in our choices?
>> What hopes did we share in common?
>> What values drove our choices?
>> How can we choose to live out the hopes we named?
>> How can we be hope for others?

Adaption

Use movie clips or movie quotes instead. Allow extra time.

Dance With Me!

 10–15 minutes

 none

Invite small teams of 3–4 to take 5 minutes to create at least 2–3 interpretive dance movements to reflect their experience. Then, have each team perform their interpretive dance. If time allows, try to merge all the dance moves into one flowing performance.

Going Deeper

» What did our dances say about our experience?
» What is a moment we want to remember?
» What moment solidified that we spent our time well?

Strengthening Reflection

Look for Ways to Engage Each Person:

Build on the strengths and personalities of your group to choose activities that will help them grow individually and collectively. Allow time to patiently nudge introverts into a place where they are comfortable sharing their thoughts, feelings and ideas. Vary your use of personal reflection, small group reflection and large group reflection. Use multiple intelligences such as music, art mediums, and nature to tap creativity. For sensitive topics, consider allowing space for anonymous comments to solicit honest, uninfluenced answers.

Emoji-Onk!

 5–10 minutes

 none

Ask participants to take 30 seconds to create an emoji face, sound (like oink or onk or honk) or movement that captures how they feel about the upcoming project (or felt about the recent experience). Take turns for everyone to share. Ask questions to clarify any confusing faces, sounds, or movements. Then dig deeper to explore their reactions. Need to simplify? Ask participants to simply draw emojis.

Going Deeper

- » Did we have similar feelings or were they all different?
- » What contributed to our responses?
- » When we serve, how should we approach people in a way that communicates genuine concern and respect?
- » What do we need to do? What attitudes should we promote?
- » What reactions would you like to see in the people we serve?

Object Share

 15–20 minutes

 find during the activity

Invite your group to take a quick 5–10-minute exploratory walk of your indoor or outdoor space to find an object that represents their individual answers to a posed reflection question related to what you're focusing on, such as—

- Find an object that represents what stood out to you about the population we worked with.
- Find an object that represents what you think you can do regarding this issue.
- Find an object that represents your understanding of the Civil War.
- Find an object that represents a tool we could use to teach others about geometry.
- Find an object that presents the presentation skill you most need to work on developing.

When time is up, have everyone gather and take turns telling about their object and viewpoint. Depending on your time, do the sharing in the big group or in smaller teams.

Option: Let participants use their backpacks to search for items.

Going Deeper

  » How hard was it to choose an object that represents your thoughts?

  » What did you learn about other people's perspectives?

  » What should our next steps be both as a group and as individuals?

Quotable Thoughts

 10–12 minutes

 selected quote

Share a quote appropriate to service, teamwork, or the problem being faced. For example: *It is better to light one small candle than to curse the darkness. —Confucius*

Use the quote to kick-off a discussion. With the example quote, a potential conversation might revolve around 1) the importance of taking action, voting, or advocating for justice instead of simply complaining; 2) acknowledging all the ways that little actions add up to have a ripple effect of change; or 3) how an historical activist offered a single flame to give hope and light in a tumultuous situation. Begin with questions such as these:

- What does this quote mean to you?
- Why might it be important for our group right now?

Pictures Reaction

 10–12 minutes

 visuals from magazines, greeting cards, photos, or images printed from online

---

Either post the visuals on walls or spread them out in piles on tables. Pose a question to the group and ask each to select an image that best represents their answer or reaction to the posed prompt. Ask the group to explain their choice and show their pictures (if not on the walls). The discussion can be facilitated within the big group, with those standing around the same image (if they're posted), or by having members pair up to talk with a partner.

Sample discussion prompts might include:

- Choose the image that best represents your role in the group today.
- Choose the image that best fits your overall reaction to what you can do to help your group be stronger or to help strengthen your community.
- Choose an image that matches your feelings about our success today.

Going Deeper

- » How did you choose your image for this activity?
- » What did you notice about the choices people made in this activity?
- » What can we learn from this activity?

Balloon Keep Up

 15–20 minutes

 4 or 6 inch balloons, skein of yarn, stopwatch

Explain that the group is going to go through a series of challenges. Give each person a balloon.

Challenge #1 is for individuals to juggle their balloons in the air for 30 seconds without dropping them or letting them hit the walls.

Challenge #2 is for pairs to juggle BOTH of their balloons in the air for 30 seconds without dropping them. Invite participants to choose their partner, and then tell the group when to start.

Challenge #3: Instruct the group to create 2 different teams with half of the members in each one. Their challenge is to attempt to juggle ALL of the balloons in the air for 30 seconds but each person can only hit any given balloon one time in a row. After 30 seconds, ask how they did. Give them 2 minutes to strategize and plan, then repeat the group juggling challenge.

Challenge #4: Invite the teams to link to become one large group and attempt to juggle all the balloons, with no drops, only hitting each balloon one time in a row for 30 seconds. Give them 2 minutes to strategize and plan, then repeat the group juggling challenge.

Going Deeper

» What was it like to juggle a balloon all by yourself? What was hard? What was easy?

» What about when you worked with a partner? What was hard? What was easy?

» What about when two people became numerous people involved? What was hard? What was easy?

» What about when the whole group got involved? What was hard? What was easy?

» What helped us get better at juggling the balloons in these early phases? What were the keys for success?

» What can we learn from this experience to apply to our work with others or in the community? Which technique will make us most successful in accomplishing our goals?

» How can we keep everyone engaged and energized for the work?

» What do we need to be mindful of as our group gets larger or tasks become more complex?

Shuffle, Shuffle

 5–8 minutes

 large space (gym, outdoors)

 Choose an open-ended reflection question for the group to answer, such as "What is one thing you look forward to in this project?" "What is one way you know our group made a difference today?" "What is one thing you learned about this topic that you can use in life?"

Divide the group, if large, into smaller teams of 10 or less. Have participants stand in a circle(s) and put their arms around (or hands on) the shoulders of the person to either side of them. Explain that you will start by giving the group a shuffling direction to follow. Once the group is moving in that direction, any player can say, "Stop!" to stop the group movement. Once the group stops, the player who said "Stop!" must give an answer to the reflection question.

After they have answered, they will tell the group which direction to shuffle next. They might say, "Shuffle left" or "Shuffle to the middle" or "Shuffle up," or in whatever creative direction they choose. At their direction, the group will shuffle until the next player says, "Stop." Repeat the process—shuffle, stop, answer, give a new shuffle direction, and so on—until everyone has had a chance to reflect aloud.

Conversation Angles
(Pre-Project)

 10–15 minutes

 none

Tell your group about the situation they are going to address, giving basic understanding and familiarity with the issue. Ask: What strikes you about this problem? What stands out about its impact? Allow time for people to answer the questions.

Have another person restate the problem aloud again in their own words. Ask: How does this problem touch your life? Allow time for people to answer the question.

Have a third person reiterate the problem for the group. Ask: What is the problem asking of us, of each of you? What can we do to alleviate suffering, stop this issue from continuing, or help out?

After a fourth and final statement of the problem by another participant, invite the group to share their vision for a world in which this issue exists no longer. The problem has been solved. Invite them to picture and reflect on what can be; then dive into possible solutions and actions the group can take to make a difference.

Practicing from the Divine

In many faith disciplines, contemplative reflection is a common practice. Often, people read a sacred text and examine it from different angles, using different questions, in an attempt to learn and grow in understanding.

As applied to service-learning experiences, such conversations will elicit richer understanding and depth as differing perspectives emerge and the group thoughtfully examines the issue. This approach to having a conversation about world issues is an adaption of lectio divina (holy reading), which is a pattern of prayer using a Bible passage.

Conversation Angles
(Post-Project)

 10–15 minutes

 none

Explain that you are going to have people take turns summarizing the experience (or topic) and that then you will ask questions to dig in deeper to what the group is taking away from it all.

Recap the experience, then ask the group: What strikes you about this experience? What stands out about what happened (or what was done or accomplished)? Allow time for people to answer the question.

Ask another volunteer to run through again what happened in their own words.

Now ask: How does this event or knowledge touch your life? How does it impact you? Allow time for answers.

Have a third person restate the narrative as they understood it. Ask: How does this incident impact others?

Ask for one last storyteller to recap the account. Ask: Is this occurrence asking anything more of you? Is there more for you to do personally? A way you should change? A place you should volunteer your time or a cause beckoning you to commit to? Is a new way of being involved asking you to take action? Is there something else to be learned? What are you being invited to do in the next 48 hours?

Skilled Relay

 15–20 minutes

 signs, tape, activity slips (enough for 1 set per team), paper clips

 Make a sign for each 21st century skill. Write the name large at the top of each sign with its definition on the back.

Definitions:

1. **Critical thinking**—the ability to think with depth and discernment about a variety of issues and subjects
2. **Creativity**—the ability to imagine, build, craft ideas and tangible items
3. **Collaboration**—the ability to work together in cooperation with everyone doing their own part
4. **Communication**—the ability to share and receive information
5. **Information literacy**—the ability to intake and interpret information
6. **Media literacy**—the ability to access information and apply it to needed situations
7. **Technology literacy**—the ability to use technology to help people and circumstances as well as accomplish tasks
8. **Flexibility**—the ability to "go with the flow"
9. **Leadership**—the ability to guide, direct, and manage a group
10. **Initiative**—the ability to appropriately take ownership of work that needs to be done and perform tasks without necessarily waiting for explicit permission or outside commands to do so

11. **Productivity**—the ability to get work done in a timely and efficient manner
12. **Social skills**—the awareness, attitude, and skills to get along with others

Tape each sign on the wall. Copy, print off, and cut up activity slips. Make 1 set per team. Paper clip each set.

Listens well

Clarifies and speaks clearly

Cooperates with others

Encourages and supports other team mates

Does fair share of work assigned

Steps in to take on something that needs to be done without being asked

---

Is willing to learn more

Tries new things easily

Adapts well

Likes to brainstorm

Picks the best solution to a problem

Knows how to create a webpage

Is comfortable working in different computer codes

Easily navigates online searches

Asks lots of questions before making a decision

Always has work done early

Knows everyone and can connect people easily

Likes to cook

Doodles to think

Enjoys woodworking or carving

Volunteers to teach or facilitate workshops

Leads icebreakers

Plays an instrument

Able to quickly search and research on the web

Uses social media venues quickly and efficiently

Engages the group or peers in problem solving

Makes sure everyone has a meaningful role

Posts pictures of events

Know the best way to navigate any side of town

Encourages others

Loves to read books

Hears an idea and digs in to learn more

Divide the group into teams. Have each team sit at a table. Give each team a paper-clipped activity set and some tape. Introduce the names of each of the categories.

Explain that based on their intuition, experience and intelligence, each team will determine where they think an activity best fits. Once they decide as a group, one person should take the activity slip and tape it on the sign they've chosen as the best fit. Only one person per team can run at a time.

When all teams are done, look at what was posted for each skill. As a group, look to see if any teams posted activities under different categories. If yes, ask whichever team(s) placed it there to talk about their thinking. Ask other teams to identify where they put theirs and tell their thinking behind their decision.

TIP

Listen for the logic behind their reasoning. There are some slips that could go in multiple spots. Affirm those choices. Also, as the facilitator, ensure that the teams' critical thinking is on track for their choices. If not, direct them to a better fit for their selection.

After the group is finished, reveal and talk about the definition for each skill. Ask teams if they would move any of their choices with the new information.

Going Deeper

» Which skill is easiest for you to use?

» Which skill is hardest for you to use? Why is that?

» What do you think you'll gain from developing each of these skills?

» How can these skills help you in groups? In classes? With projects?

» What skills or knowledge are you looking forward to practicing or gaining in this group?

» You have been practicing three skills: 1. being intentional about reflecting, 2. assessing your own strengths, and 3. evaluating where you want to work to be better. How do you think those skills will help you be better equipped for future work?

Opposite Ends

 10–15 minutes

 choose your word/phrase pair

 Choose from the paired list below or create your own word pairing to use as your reflection question.

- Cartoon or documentary
- Youtube video or podcast
- A series of "likes" or a series of "shares"
- Candy Crush or Solitaire
- Main meal or dessert (or appetizer)
- Cliff notes version or actual book
- Surfing waves or surfing the web
- Playing Connect Four or playing chess
- Building a sand castle or building a Jenga® tower
- Riding a horse or riding a motorcycle

Have the group gather in the middle of your space. Explain that you're going to state aloud two choices and point to one side of the room for each choice. Everyone should vote with their feet and stand on the side of the room that best reflects their response to the question posed. Remind the group that their choice is totally from their perspective. There is no right or wrong answer. Their response is simply how they interpret and connect the choice to the question.

Example: "Was the classroom experience today more like playing connect four or playing chess?" Point to one side of the room as you say, "playing connect four," and point to the other side of the room as you say, "playing chess." Instruct them to go stand on the side of the space that best fits their answer.

Once everyone has chosen a side, then ask a few people to tell why they answered the way they did. If desired, choose a new pairing and ask a new question.

Going Deeper
  » Why do you think we had different reactions and yet went through the same experience?
  » How do our different perspectives enrich our understanding of the experience?

Rock, Paper, Scissors Reflection

 15–20 minutes

 reflection questions

 write the reflection questions on a board or have a copy on hand

---

Have the group form a loose circle. The activity begins in the fashion of the traditional Rock, Paper, Scissors game with everyone beating one fist into their other open palm as they count 1, 2, 3; on 3, everyone chooses independently to throw down either the rock, paper, or scissors motion. (Rock is a fist, paper is the hand flattened out, and scissors are the upheld index and middle fingers, a.k.a, the peace sign fingers.)

Once the 3-count is called, everyone should form and maintain their choice as they look around to try to gather with 2 other people who chose a different element from theirs.

The goal is to form groups of 3 that include one complete set of rock, paper, and scissors.

If groups form, have them step to the side. They're set. Play another round or so with the rest of the participants, until all groups have formed. (Note: if you stop here, you now have an icebreaker that divides your group into smaller teams for any purpose.)

Once all trios are established, they sit down to talk about their reflection question, which is based on the element they chose when their small group formed. You may adapt questions as desired to fit an issue facing the school, place of faith, after-school program, or group or for taking about current events or issues, etc.

Rock, Paper, Scissors Trio Discussion Questions

- **Rock beats scissors**. What is an obstacle or challenge you overcame today? What is something you beat?
- **Scissors cut paper.** How did you begin to cut through an injustice today? How did you cut down the issue or cut through misunderstandings to better understand the truth of the problem?
- **Paper covers rock.** Whom did you protect today? How did you help put a barrier between the issue and those impacted by that issue? In what ways can you now wrap your head around this issue that you couldn't before?

Going Deeper
　》　Ask for a few thoughts from each group about what they shared.

Comfort Levels

 15–20 minutes

 statements

Demonstrate the positions for each statement that will be read aloud. People will answer according to their comfort level:

- If they are really comfortable, they are "walking proud" and they should simply walk in place to show their comfort.
- If the statement means that what happens is a "stretch" for them, they should simply stretch their arms out to the side or overhead (don't hit the person next to them!).
- If they aren't comfortable at all, then participants should curl in with their bodies assuming a "fetal position" to show they are shrinking away from what is read.

Have the group practice each motion together before reading the statements aloud. Explain that these statements reflect a variety of situations the group may encounter in a service experience. A sample list is included below. Feel free to add or adapt statements to make them more specific to your group's focus or the activity involved.

How comfortable are you...
- Interacting with strangers
- Asking for help

- Voicing a question if you don't understand
- Getting dirty
- Getting wet
- Being in the hot sun for hours
- Doing a task you may not enjoy
- Doing a task you have never done before or aren't good at it
- Picking up trash
- Stuffing envelopes
- Hammering nails
- Being artistic
- Receiving feedback if you don't do something right
- Making mistakes
- Showing compassion or empathy
- Working with adults
- Working with youth
- Working with people you don't know
- Working with people different from you in any kind of way (abilities, skin tone, accents, body shape, etc.)
- Working under pressure

Ask what other pertinent fears and concerns they would add to this list. With each answer, ask for the group to demonstrate their comfort level.

Going Deeper

Facing new situations, people, environments and tasks can bring out a lot of different emotions. Sometimes those emotions might conflict. We can feel excited and scared at the same time. We can feel threatened and brave. So many emotions!

» What feelings were dominant for you as you went through this activity?

- » What did you learn about yourselves as you think through everything you felt?
- » Are we comfortable overall as a group?
- » Are we ready to face what we'll be doing or is there something more we need to work on to prepare?
- » What were the major areas where we're not comfortable?
- » What can we do to increase our comfort level in that area?

Lucky Numbers Throw Down

 10–15 minutes

 none

Invite participants to find a partner. Each person will bounce their fist into the palm of their other hand three times as they would when playing Rock, Paper, Scissors. (Review instructions on page 97 if you need a refresher on how to play Rock, Paper, Scissors.) On the third bounce, everyone throws down a number, choosing from 1–5. Do a practice round.

Explain that you will give the instructions and the topic for each round of play. Pairs will have 1 minute to discuss. Have pairs do their throw down, then share answers to the question for round one. After one minute, invite participants to find a new partner for a new round. Continue the pattern of throw down, share and mingle until all 5 topics have been discussed.

Round 1: Pairs take the higher number of the two numbers and come up with that many things they are proud of from the day.

Round 2: Pairs take the lower number of the two numbers and talk about what they learned from the day.

Round 3: Pairs add the two numbers together and tell what they now know for fact about the issue.

Round 4: Pairs subtract the numbers and give that number of reasons the issue is an important one to address.

Round 5: Pairs pick one of the two numbers and come up with possible further action steps related to the issue.

Going Deeper

» What did you learn from the experience that you don't want to forget?

» What do you now know that you didn't before?

» How is your thinking different moving forward?

» What ideas do you have for what we should do next?

Book Ends

 15–20 minutes

 pre-written beginning and ending index cards, writing utensils, recorder

 Write out one beginning and one ending on each index card

Beginnings:
- It was a dark and stormy night...
- Once upon a time...
- In a galaxy far, far away...
- Space, the final frontier...
- At the beginning of time...
- Many moons ago...
- All fairy tales have a beginning. This is one of them...
- This is the story of our people...

Endings:
- As they rode into the sunset, you could hear them say...
- And the monster was never seen again...
- And all was well until...
- The book of knowledge was lost, or was it...
- The clock struck midnight and...
- Peace seemed to reign again...

- They pictured their days would always be this…
- They were the world's last hope for peace. They failed. Now, they rebuild…

Divide the group into teams of 3. Distribute writing utensils and a beginning and ending index card to each group. Explain that their task is to create a short story of their experience (on the project, with the topic, or in service). The story must include

1) a beginning (at least 2-3 sentences),
2) a middle that illustrates an arc of change (either how they've personally changed, how they situation which the group tackled has been changed or how someone else who was involved in the project changed as a result of actions taken by this group)
3) and the story must have an end (at least 2-3 sentences).

Give the group 15 minutes to work. As each team tells their stories, record them. Stories can then be shared with others or used as part of celebration events. Written copies can also be used in news or reflective articles.

Going Deeper

» Think about your beginning of this service experience. What did you come into this project thinking it would be like? What was your attitude coming in?

» At what point during the service day did you arc? Where did that change take place: Was it in your attitude? your knowledge of the problem? your understanding of the difference you could make? What was that middle for you when things began to change?

» The day has ended, but has your service story ended? If yes, how will you label the ending? What was the conclusion?
» If your service story hasn't ended, what do you think the sequel will be? What's next?

Reflection Trivia

 15–20 minutes

 paper, pens

Divide participants into small teams of 4–6. Instruct each team to come up with 3 questions regarding the experience they've undertaken from start to finish. (The experience might be learning more about an issue, completing a task together, doing a service project, finishing a unit on women suffrage, or the group bonding together.) This activity allows you, the leader, to check for understanding and identify where points may not have been understood completely.

The questions that the participants come up with should be answerable by anyone present during the event, orientation, training, or meeting referenced and must be from what the group underwent as a whole (what was learned, experienced, funny moments, etc.). Give them 5 minutes to come up with their questions.

Once done, have teams partner with two other teams. One team poses one of their questions to the other teams. The first person from one of the other teams to "buzz" in (rattle keys, hit the table or raise their hand) with the correct answer receives a round of applause. (Points system is optional.)

Teams have 5 seconds to buzz in to answer or the questioning team gives their answer. Each team asks all of their questions before another team takes the questioning role. Repeat until all teams have asked their questions.

Going Deeper

  » As a big group, ask if anyone had a unique question or really interesting question posed that they want to share?
  » What, if any, themes emerged in the questions asked? What was key to the group experience?
  » What key takeaways were mentioned? What will people remember most?

Head / Heart / Hands / Feet

 15–20 minutes

 chart paper, markers, blank paper, writing utensils

 Make drawings on chart paper and write out the following prompts:

- **Head**: What new knowledge did you gain today? (about self, the community, the topic, or the issue)
- **Heart**: What fed your heart today?
- **Hand**: What skills did you wrap your hands around today and use?
- **Feet**: Given what you now know, what action will you take?

Show the group the listed questions. Ask them to think about each one and doodle or write out their answers. Give them 5–10 minutes to work. Then invite them to find at least one other person with whom to share their responses. If you have time, as a big group, follow up with the Going Deeper questions.

Going Deeper

» What do you value most about what you experienced as a change agent?

- » What knowledge do you value?
- » Which of your skills made you the most proud?
- » What accomplishment makes you smile?
- » What do you want to learn more about?
- » What do you want to do next with your new understanding?
- » How can our group support you if your next work differs from the direction the group wants to take?

Sticky Note Successes & Challenges

 15–25 minutes

 sticky notes, writing utensils, flip chart, marker

 Label two flip-chart sheets: one with a smiley face and one with a sad face.

Ask the group to reflect on their successes and their challenges and write them out, one per Post-it® note. Collect the successes and place them on the smiley face sheet. Place the challenges on the sad face one. Quickly categorize the responses by placing similar ideas together. Celebrate a success and then collectively collaborate on identifying 2–3 solutions for one of the identified challenges. Repeat process: celebrate a success and then work together to solve a challenge.

TIP

If the group is too large to debrief, divide into smaller teams and recruit leaders to keep teams on track. Have all teams go through the activity at the same time, then have the full group do a gallery walk (walking around the room to view each team's results posted on the wall) of the results.

Going Deeper

- » What idea did you hear as we brainstormed solutions to challenges that appealed to you?
- » What tactic do you want to try against a challenge you face?
- » What was a celebration moment that made you smile?
- » How does celebrating successes, great or small, help us persevere?
- » How does the support of others help us continue despite difficulties?
- » What do you want to remember from this activity?

Zoom In / Zoom Out

 15–25 minutes

 paper, writing utensils

Ask each participant to sketch out with drawings or words what they think the bigger picture is regarding this project (topic, idea, or lesson concept). What's the vision? What are they working towards? Give them 5–8 minutes to work. Then, discuss (and they can also share their drawings if they want to do so).

Adapt the questions below as needed to fit your focus:
- How does what we are doing on this project relate to our mission as a group?
- How does it connect to our goals? How does this project help the school/agency/community we're working with achieve its goals?
- How does it link to the agency/community's priorities?
- How does what we're doing help other people on an individual level?

Tell the group, "This is the zoom out perspective with its teachings. It captures the bigger picture much like a wide-angle lens on a camera. Now, let's look at what the zoom in lesson is. Zooming in shows closer details of what makes up that bigger picture. Zooming in can show details and nuances that aren't always visible from afar."

Now ask the group to zoom in on what they think needs to happen to achieve their vision. Ask them to sketch out with drawings or words their ideas for what they think they need to do or how they can give body to the vision. Allow another 5–8 minutes for the group to work.

When the time is up, invite volunteers to identify details that stood out to them. Encourage discussion around their insights and ideas.

Going Deeper

» What are the tasks we need to do to pull off our vision?

» What needs to happen in order for us to do our project well?

» What questions do we need answered? Where do we need coaching?

» Where do we need to clarify specific goals we have: what the tasks are, the timelines, who is responsible for each task and with whom we will be working?

» How does what we do in each of our jobs or assigned tasks matter? Why does zooming in to be clear and do a good job on the small details matter?

Die Review

 15–20 minutes

 dice

Ask for a volunteer to roll a die. The number rolled is the number of people who will answer a posed question. Roll the die again. This number indicates which question each person will answer:

1. What did you learn today?

2. What was your favorite moment?

3. What was challenging?

4. What skill muscles did you work today?

5. Where do you see an opportunity for improving something (in self or how something is done) to address this issue?

6. Where did you (or how could you) consider an obstacle/ challenge encountered from another person's perspective?

Repeat the process multiple times to cover all the questions. If desired, use a pair of dice and increase the number of question options for people to answer on the second roll. Turn the questions into a review of content to be used as a pre-test for the topic that will be covered the next day, or use in place of a formal quiz.

Spinning Success

 10–15 minutes

 brad, cardstock print out of spinner questions

 Print out spinner questions on page 118 onto cardstock. Attach a brad (the spinning arrow game piece) to the spinner grid by making a small hole in the middle of the grid and pushing the brad through it. Or, buy a game spinner online and use the

Spinning Success Questions:

1. Value from the day
2. I learned…
3. A skill I developed
4. Best part of the experience
5. Favorite part of the project
6. Biggest area of growth
7. A contribution I made
8. I am most proud of how I…

Ask the group to reflect on their group project from the very beginning to now. Taking turns, have each person spin the spinner (brad) and answer the question indicated by where its arrow points.

Going Deeper

» What do you see possible for yourself now that your team has completed this project?
» What can you imagine that you didn't before?
» How can you apply what you've learned from working on this project to other areas of life?
» How has what you've learned helped you grow as a person?
» How has what you've learned helped your understanding of this topic or issue?

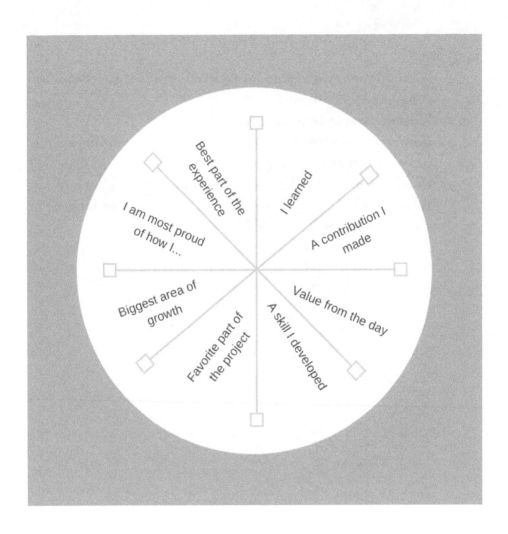

Best part of the experience

I learned

I am most proud of how I...

A contribution I made

Biggest area of growth

Value from the day

Favorite part of the project

A skill I developed

Spinning Success, Too

 10–15 minutes

 brad, cardstock print out of spinner questions

 Print out spinner questions on page 121 onto cardstock. Attach a brad (the spinning arrow game piece) to the spinner grid by making a small hole in the middle of the grid and pushing the brad through it. Or, buy a game spinner online and use these questions:

1. Biggest cheerleader
2. A way a teammate helped me
3. A shout out to…because they…
4. What I'll take with me
5. I can now do…
6. I now know…
7. People who can help me move on
8. Next I want to…

Tell the group that part of taking on new challenges is gaining. We gain ideas, knowledge, experience, skills, and support; sometimes we even gain new friendships. What have they gained from their experience together?

Taking turns, have each person spin the spinner and answer the question indicated by where the arrow is pointing.

Going Deeper

> » What "gain" do you value most from your experience?
> » What have you learned from everything you've "gained?"
> » As we reflect on it all, do the "gains" point us toward a natural next step as a group? As individuals? (Depending on your focus, you might want to prompt thinking such as the next steps the might take, careers to explore, or ways to get involved in the community, to work more on a project or issue, etc.)
> » What will we do next to keep moving forward?

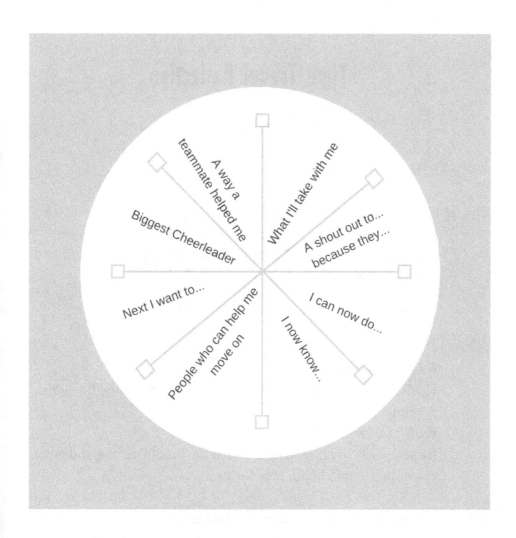

Reprinted with permission from **Great Group Reflections: 60 Compelling Challenges to Prompt Self-Discovery & Critical Thinking** *Copyright ©2019 by Susan Ragsdale and Ann Saylor. All rights reserved.*

Time Travel Reflection

 15–20 minutes

 chart paper, markers, paper, writing utensils

 List the word "What" along with its categories and their descriptions on chart paper:

What?

- **Knew**: what you knew
- **Skills**: skills already known plus what you hoped to learn, develop, or practice
- **Fears**: what you feared
- **Hopes**: what you hoped the experience would be like and what you hoped would happen by the end

Distribute paper and writing utensils. Explain that the group is going to time travel through their group experience, starting with their pre-working together selves all the way to imagining their futures. To start, ask everyone to focus on their pre-group involvement selves as they think through each of the different categories listed on the chart paper. Have them jot down answers to each category on their papers, describing who they were and what they knew before the group got together.

Next invite participants to think now about their current, post-experience selves. Invite them to think in terms of "So What?"

Ask them to show by thumb signal (i.e., thumbs up for yes, thumbs sideways (so-so or somewhat) or thumbs down for no) their initial response to these posed questions:

So What?

- Has your knowledge increased or stayed the same compared to your pre-group self (thumbs up or thumbs sideways)?
- Did you learn what you wanted to learn?
- Did you learn things you didn't expect?
- Did you practice skills you knew you had?
- Did you develop new skills?
- Were those skills the ones you hoped to learn or further develop?
- Did any of your fears become real?
- Did any of your hopes for what you envisioned the experience pan out the way you thought they might?
- Did you develop a new sense of hope from what you experienced during this project?
- Did what you hoped would happen by service end happen?
- If no, did that end up being a good thing?

Finally, ask the group to think about their future selves as they answer these "Now What?" prompts.

Now What?

- What can you now do that you couldn't before?
- What new knowledge have you gained that will help you in future life experiences?
- Of what are you most proud?
- What are your hopes for your next experience?
- How do you hope you are different?
- What change do you hope to create?

Reflection Scramble

 15–20 minutes

 question cards, scissors

 Prepare question cards. Place question cards face down in the middle of a table. Use the questions below or create more project specific ones of your own. If using these questions, simply copy and cut apart.

How did our project impact the issue?

What was my role?

How did my work fit into the bigger picture?

Was this service project something I could do by myself?
Why or why not?

How did what we did improve the situation?

_____

What about the experience did I value most?

_____

What is the agency's greatest contribution to the community?

_____

What about this issue bothers me?

_____

Why does working on this particular issue appeal to me?

_____

Working on this project, what I got really clear on
regarding the issue was...

_____

Working on this project, what I got really clear on regarding my own
abilities to make a difference was...

_____

Divide the group into two teams. Have each team stand in a line behind different sides of a table facing each other. The first person from each team competes against each other. Explain that after the card in the middle is flipped over and read aloud, the first person to grab the card and answer the question truthfully wins the card for their team.

Have new team members step up for the next round of questions. Continue playing rounds until all cards have been answered.

This activity can be stretched out to use as pre, during and post-reflection exercises. Additionally, craft questions to fit the What? So What? Now What? phases.

This One! This One!

 15–25 minutes

 assortment of random items (such as tennis balls, can opener, fidgets, buckets, measuring spoons, magic markers, eraser, staples, building blocks, pens, superhero figurines, and play dough)

Place the supplies on the middle of a table. Ask everyone to take a seat around the table. Ask them to think of which item best represents their answer for the posed question. Pick one from below or create your own.

- Which item best represents your contribution to the group work today?
- Which item best represents the experience overall?
- Which item best represents the most prominent value demonstrated during the group experience?
- Which item best represents the group's accomplishments?
- Which item best represents an example of how you saw change being played out during our activity?

After the question is given, instruct everyone to select an item. Then, taking turns, invite each person to hold up their item and share their thoughts about why they chose what they did and how it best relates to the query. "I picked this one because ..." Challenge the group to listen closely to one another and ask any questions to further draw out deeper insights or further explore stories heard.

Repeat process with a new question after items are placed back in the middle of the table. Do as often as desired. Optionally, you could mix up the questions and item selections to use over multiple sessions.

Social Sharing

 5–10 minutes

 ball or paper wad, music, music source (app on a phone, computer, IPAD, or radio), speakers (if needed)

Set the stage by saying that on social media, people often respond to what's said or seen by using three tools: like, comment, or share. Explain that the group is going to use that same format to reflect on what happened (or the lesson plan, etc.).

Gather the group in a circle. Give one person the ball. Explain that music will be playing and when the music stops, whoever has the ball must respond the prompt you give, which will either be—

- **Like:** Something you liked from this experience.
- **Comment**: A comment you want to make related to the experience (Stay focused!). Or,
- **Share**: Something you will share with someone who wasn't part of this.

Whether the ball is tossed around in the circle or randomly thrown is up to you as the facilitator. You know your group.

Start the music and go through the first round. Once the participant has finished talking, explain that speakers will get to choose one of the three responses for the next person to answer when the music stops. Repeat for 5–8 minutes until everyone has had a chance to respond or until the energy starts to wane.

Cereal Words Race

 15–25 minutes

 round cereal pieces (such as Cheerios) or a bag of dried beans (use if people have allergies), paper, pens

---

Invite the participants to think about their take-way from their joint experience. What did they learn? What skills did they practice? How are they more knowledgeable? Ask them to each jot down a word on scrap paper without showing anyone else. Gather all answers from participants. Shuffle papers.

Divide the group into 2–4 competing teams. Have each team gather around a table with a pile of cereal in the center of each table.

Instruct teams to send one participant to you, the facilitator. Show them all one of the reflection words. Next, instruct the word spellers to race back to their team and spell out the word using the cereal. The goal is to be the first team to correctly guess the word being spelled out. Award one point to the winning team.

Continue play, with a new team member and a new word for each round, until everyone has had a chance to go or until the allotted time runs out. Be sure to save time for the debriefing. Remember to have each team share their words aloud at the end of each round. At the end of the spell-out time, announce which team earned the most points.

Going Deeper

» What words best captured the experience for you?

» What word was or is most relevant to you? Why?

» Did any of these words trigger other memories related to our experience? Share what word(s) and memory came to mind, and why.

» What words come to mind when you think about our group and how we relat to each other? Why?

» What words remind you of good experiences our group has had together?

» What words remind you of some ways our group needs to grow more?

» What is a word you want others to associate with you?

3-2-1 Gratitude Journal

 15–20 minutes

 paper. writing utensils

Have the group sit in a circle with enough space for papers to be placed in the middle of the circle. Distribute paper and a writing utensil to each person. Instruct them to put a line of 6 dots along the left side of their paper. Explain that the group is going to create a 3–2–1 reflection countdown. Everyone will jot down three things they are grateful for in regards to the group's experience together for each of the first three dots, writing one idea out across from each dot. When they're done, they should put their paper upside down in the center of the circle and take another person's paper when it's available.

This time, after reading what's written on the paper they have, they add two more things they were grateful for related to the group's experiences. (The idea is that reading what others are grateful for might inspire or remind people of other things they are grateful for). Then, they place their paper in the middle and wait for a new paper to take.

The group repeats the process a third time adding a final gratitude to the remaining dot after reading all the ideas on their new paper. At this point, all six dots should have something written beside them.

Have group members find their original papers. Give them time to review their newly formed list. Invite participants to find a partner (other than the person sitting to their immediate left or right) and share some of the feedback from their papers. Allow 2–3 minutes.

Going Deeper

» As you thought about the things you are grateful for from this experience, what stood out?

» What were some of the little things you were grateful for that meant a lot?

» What were some of the big things?

» What person(s) came to mind? Why?

» How did reading other people's gratitudes affect you?

Puzzle Statements

 10–20 minutes

 2 pictures of the team printed on cardstock, scissors, painters tape

 Cut each picture into 12-20 puzzle pieces, being careful to keep the pieces for each puzzle separate. Keep one piece back from each puzzle and set them aside (in a pocket or notebook) to use with the reflection discussion. Place the rest of each puzzle set face down on the table with plenty of space between the two sets so each team can work easily. Mark a starting line 5'-10' away from the table.

Divide the group into two teams of 3–10. Have teams line up relay style behind the starting line. At the signal, the first person from each team runs to the table, turns over all the puzzle pieces in their particular puzzle, and joins two pieces together. After making that initial connection, the person runs back and tags the next person in line. The next person runs to the table and makes another link, then runs back. Repeat the relay until both teams reach the end of their puzzle artwork (completed except for their final missing pieces).

Ask immediately: Did you complete the challenge? Why or why not? (Reinforce: A puzzle piece was missing!) Acknowledge the missing pieces and tell them that as a group that we're going to use the puzzles with their missing pieces as an analogy for reflection.

Going Deeper

- » How did your team work together?
- » What, if anything, was missing in your teamwork?
- » What was missing from this overall experience that would have challenged you more?
- » What piece (hold up a puzzle piece) did exploring this topic offer you? In other words, what did you learn or gain?
- » What piece did the group offer you?
- » What piece did you most value about the experience?
- » What piece do you want to always remember or honor? What's your takeaway?
- » Say: "These pictures are not complete. Something is missing. If you hadn't been in the picture during this experience, the group would have been incomplete."
- » What piece did you bring to this experience?
- » What skills did you use? How did you make tasks go smoother? Who did you help?
- » What connection did you see between your contribution and what others did?
- » What piece will you bring to any place you are a part of?

If time, ask participants to speak out about the contributions they heard/observed/saw contributed by others.

At Their Best

 20–30 minutes

 chart paper, markers, tape

 Identify a person (generic or specific) or group of people for participants to discuss. For example, you could choose a book character (such as Harry Potter) or a leader being studied (such as the Dalai Lama). Or, if selecting a generic person, you could pick a category like country presidents or a career role (such as IT Tech Specialist), depending on your session's focus.

Next, decide if each team will focus on the exact same person or group of people, or if you would prefer for each team to tackle different persons or groups of people. For example, perhaps you give each team a different character from Avengers. Or you distribute a different group of people to each team who is involved in an environmental crisis you've been examining, such as the city council, farmers, business leaders, etc.

Divide the group into smaller teams of 3–5. Give supplies to each group. Assign an At Their Best! focus person (or people group) to each team.

Explain that teams will have 10 minutes to create At Their Best! posters. Instruct them to draw out on chart paper their person (or people group), and then identify the qualities, skills, attitudes, and values they see within their assigned person. Challenge them to use more pictures than words.

As they create, they should think about and discuss these questions first:

What does it take to be the best _____ ever? What attitude does that person (or group) have? What qualities do they possess? What do they value? What are their strengths, gifts, and talents?

Give teams 10 minutes to work together on their creations. Note when two minutes are remaining and have groups determine what they will share about their work when it's their turn to report.

Have teams hang their posters on the wall or set them on a table. Do a gallery walk (with everyone walking from poster to poster) to view each creation. Have each team present key qualities from their discussion as the group views their particular piece. If possible, allow time for the bigger group to ask questions.

Going Deeper

- » What common themes did you notice among the different posters?
- » What qualities do you aspire to exhibit yourself?
- » How easy will it be for you to show up each day as your best self? Do you think you can do that? Why or why not?
- » What qualities do you want others to see in you? How can you make sure you show those qualities in how you live and work,

in how you interact with others, and in how you approach each day?

» How can you be YOUR best and allow others to be their best, even when those "bests" seem to be at odds?

Grab the Ball

 25–30 minutes

 paper wad or ball

Divide the group into smaller teams of 4. Instruct each team to come up with 4 or 5 topic-related questions in the style of "answer the question" or "true or false" statements, each with a certain point value. Give them 8 minutes to work.

When done, have 2 teams cluster around a table. Place a ball in the center of the table within equal, reachable distance of the ball.

Ask for one of the other teams to volunteer to be the game leaders. Instruct the game-leading team to take turns reading one of their questions or true/false statements. The first player to grab the ball must answer accordingly (answer the question or decide if a statement is true or false and give a reason why or reword the statement so that it IS true). The rest of the group (those not playing and the game-leading team) decide if the player gets the assigned point value or not.

Continue play until one team wins. Switch roles for competing teams and game-leading teams.

Choices

 15–20 minutes

 appropriate props to emphasize the discussion point

Set out before your group the props essential to the discussion. Space them around in a circle on the floor or on a table.

For example, a lesson looking at homelessness, economics or history, you might include a bus pass, a water bottle, a side from a cardboard box, a pair of gloves or hat, and a fast-food restaurant coupon.

Have each one identify in their heads which item they think would be most important if they were displaced. Have them then sit around their object of choice in the circle. (Facilitator's Note: It's okay if several in the group pick the same object and you have to adjust your circle. You simply want to be able to visually see which objects participants initially pick.)

One at a time, invite the group to begin to tell a story of the object they selected. The next person builds on the previous story or starts a new story about the object they chose if it differs.

Have each story circle report out some of what they thought about during their storytelling. Then debrief asking what they know about being displaced for fact; what they don't know for fact; what they're curious about; and, what they imagine it would be like.

If needed or time allows, you can further prompt their empathy by asking them to think about and name the various activities and provisions they have during a normal day and then contrast their day to what they would do or have if they didn't have a home. How would the two listings differ?

That's Useful

 10–15 minutes

 paper, writing utensils, chart paper, markers

 Write out for all to see: What did you learn? From whom—one another, the leader, the experience, others?

Divide the group into teams of 4. Invite them to talk about the different things they've learned related to today. Instruct them to create a list of the useful things they learned and note where they learned it: one another, leader, the experience, or others.

As an example to prompt their memories, ask them to consider tying their shoes, shooting a basketball, or counting to 10. Did they learn that on their own, from a teacher, a friend, a parent, a sibling? Who taught them that useful skill?

Give them 3 minutes to craft their list of things they've learned and identifying from whom.

When time is up, have them talk about how what they learned is useful and when or where they can use that information. Give them 2–3 minutes to chat.

Ask for teams to share aloud some of what they talked about.

Going Deeper

» What's their takeaway?
» What insight did they gain from identifying the "from whom"?
» What did they learn that they didn't realize they learned until asked to reflect on it?
» How were their takeways different? The same?
» What do they most want to remember from today?

OWL

 5–15 minutes

 Owl stuffed animal (optional), chart paper & markers (optional)

 If desired, write the OWL acronym and its meaning on chart paper.

Ask the group gather in a circle. Note that owls are used as messengers in Harry Potter world. They are the links in communication for conveying information, knowledge, and wisdom. Explain that each participant is going to impart learning and wisdom by using an OWL.

State that an OWL represents—
   O—Oh, I didn't know that!
   W—Wow! That's amazing!
   L—I Love how this worked.

Starting with the first person, hand them the owl (if using it) and ask them to voice what their own OWL is. Continue to the next participant in the circle until everyone has shared.

Note collectively the similarities and differences in what everyone has learned, thought amazing, and loves.

Tᴉᴘ

The L is flexible depending on what you are doing. L can represent
"1 thing I can do to show Love to others/in this situation" if a service
project was done. Or, L might mean "I Love this part of the lesson/this
moment in history, etc." for a learning based unit.

Word Play

 5–20 minutes

 index cards, writing utensils, dictionary

 Create Word Play cards by writing out a word and its definition—one word per index card.

Create the word bank. In this example, the words reflect things associated with a job.

Example word list: payroll, supervisor, corporate culture, on-boarding, punctuality, feedback, input, timeframe, protocol, professional, professional tone (i.e., "code switching" from talking to peer to talking to a supervisor or even a customer), PTO (paid time off)

Explain that the group will explore some of the everyday vernacular of the agencies they'll be working with that they may or may not know. Words might include acronyms or simply words "normal" to work life.

Divide the group into teams of 2–4. Distribute a different word to each team. Give teams 3-4 minutes to come up with how they will demonstrate their word to the rest of the group: mime (acting it out but without the words), role playing, or giving 4 clues related to the word that might help others to guess what it is. Once time is up, have teams take turns presenting their word.

Going Deeper

To wrap up after all presentations, go through the words again. Clarify meaning and discuss relevance as needed to ensure understanding has been achieved. Ask for questions or knowledge participants might have with any given word. For example, if the word is "supervisor," ask about any experiences they've had with good supervisors or what they hope their supervisor will be like.

This game can be played all in one session to introduce new concepts and ideas or over time at various check-in's as a review or to introduce a new idea/topic for discussion.

Daily Rankings

 10–15 minutes

 paper, writing utensils

Ask the group to jot down on paper the categories you call out as they think about the experience (or topic explored). Call out the following prompts:

- major tasks
- interactions
- expectations
- accomplishments

Give them 1–2 minutes to jot down a couple of words for each category to reflect what comes to mind.

Next, ask the group to individually rank each of the four items based on their experience of the day. Was it positive, negative or a neutral moment? Instruct them to use "+" for positive, "-" for negative and "n" for neutral.

Ask: In the category you marked as positive, what were some of the things that made you identify it as positive? What made those moments good?

Next, have them consider the items they ranked negatively. Ask: Why were these items negative? Challenge the group to consider what they could do to flip those moments into neutral or even positive recollections. What could they do to change them? What actions could they take?

Finally, have the group "flip" perspectives to consider what happened from a different point of view:

What if they were the _____ (insert whoever is relevant to the situation—the teacher, the person in the story, the volunteer coordinator at the agency where they are volunteering)?

- What would their perspective be if they were in that role?
- How can they look at those moments from a different angle to see it from the other person's side?
- With that new perspective, what might they learn to apply next time if a similar situation occurs?

Artistic Honorees

 25–30 minutes

 paper, writing utensils

Distribute supplies to each person. Ask everyone to write their name at the top of the paper, then give their paper to the facilitator.

Divide the group into clusters of 4 to sit together.

As the facilitator, shuffle the papers and redistribute them randomly. Give everyone a moment to make sure they know the person on the sheet they are holding AND that they don't have the one with their own name on it or anyone else in their cluster. If during any exchange of papers a participant doesn't know the person well, they can discreetly trade papers with someone else in another cluster.

Invite everyone to write down on their person's paper underneath their name—

- one adjective that describes that person.

Have participants pass their papers to the person on their left within their cluster so that each one has a new person to consider as they answer this question—

- What is one word that expresses a skill or talent or gift this person brings to the group (or the world)?

Once again small teams pass to the left to redistribute papers so each individual has a new person. Ask the participants to record—

- One word that expresses a hope for that person's future.

Once done, have members in the cluster work together—in pairs or individually—to write a fun, positive Haiku about all 4 people they have commented on. Give the group 10 minutes to work and to share with one another. When time is up, ask for clusters to read aloud their favorite Haiku. Then have them gift their works to each of their people. Ask for any more volunteers to read aloud what they received.

Option: Instead of writing multiple individual pieces, have each member name their person and read aloud the words for that individual. After sharing each list, use all the descriptors (twelve) to create a collage of words with pictures, Haiku, song, or poem to honor ALL the names listed on their papers. When time is up, have each cluster of four perform their creative work.

Applaud and acknowledge the collective creativity and gifts of individuals and teams.

Going Deeper

- » What did you enjoy most about this activity: thinking about what you like about someone else, creating your presentation, or doing it?
- » How does it feel to have these thoughtful reflections read aloud?

» What was it like for each of you personally to hear the positive attributes that others named within you?
» What do you hope people will say about you or see in you?
» How might it impact others if you continue to look for and name the good you see within them? What effect might that have on you?
» What can you take away from this experience?

Cereal Spellers

 10–20 minutes

 round cereal pieces (such as Cheerios) or a bag of dried beans (use if people have allergies), index cards, writing utensil, timer

 Create a word bank to use in this game. Choose words that are related to your group's experience together, such as getting ready to investigate a community problem, learn more about an agency, or exploring aspects of leadership.

For example, if looking into careers, acronyms related to organizations might be your focus: CEO, CFO, VP, ASAP, BCC... If talking about service-learning, then focusing on its steps could be helpful: investigation, preparation, action, reflection, demonstration, and evaluation.

Choose words that will be relevant as the group talks about the meaning of the words. Write one word per index card.

Ask for volunteers and give each one a word card and a handful of cereal. They have 45 seconds to try to spell out their word. Instruct the rest of the group to ignore the spellers while they work. When time is up, have the group move from word to word to see if they can guess what word was being spelled out. Then, move into a discussion of the words and what they mean.

This Going Deeper example models a possible conversation based on what a group might talk about if they are preparing for summer time or first time jobs. We included it here to illustrate how relevance is drawn in by noting the "code" language that we all develop, and then playing off of that fact to dive into a conversation.

Going Deeper

Say something like this: "With your friends, you sometimes have a "code" or language particular to you. As you engage more broadly in the community with other people and organizations, you will see different "codes and languages" come into play—traditions, styles, preferences, systems, protocols, and even words used.

- » Can you share an example from now or history of how you have seen this within people, groups, or organizations?
- » What do you do or what have you done if you don't understand the "codes and languages" that you see? (Prompt if needed: when you don't understand, ask what something means. Asking shows you're interested and want to learn.)
- » What "codes and languages" are part of our group? How can we help others "decode" and better understand and integrate into our group?

T/F Block Chase

 5–15 minutes

 2 alphabet blocks: the T and the F, tape, sticky notes (for Prep Option #2), writing utensils (for Prep Option #2)

 There are two options for prep.

Option 1: Write out ahead of time statements you want the group to explore. Statements must be made for a True or False answer.

Or,

Option 2: During the activity, ask everyone to write down one assumption or truth regarding the subject of focus on a sticky note so that participants have to guess when they hear the statement whether it is true or false.

If choosing this option, give them 2 minutes to record facts or assumptions (ask them to lightly mark in the corner of their sticky at the top whether their statement is true or false). Collect statements at the end of 2 minutes.

Here are some pre-made statements samples for a variety of topics to get your brain thinking:

- **It's a big deal to be late to class.**
  True. You get a demerit if late to class.
- **Fridays are designated as casual Fridays at the job where I work so I can wear jeans.**
  This may be true or may be false. It depends on the policy of the agency where participants are working. This is fact that employees must ask questions to find out for themselves.
- **I can't get fired from a summer job.**
  False. You can get fired. Do your job and do it well. You want to do well.
- **I can't use my cell phone in my after-school program like I do at home.**
  True. While in our program space, you stay focused primarily on what we're doing in the group.
- **3 x 30 = 90.**
  True.
- **"Hola" means "goodbye" in Spanish.**
  False. It means "hello."
- **My boss wouldn't understand my situation even if I explained it.**
  False. Don't make assumptions about other people. Conversations are important. If you can't get to work on time because you're taking care of your little brother and can't leave until mom gets home, explain that to your supervisors. Let them know you want to be there but have this obstacle to work around. See if they'll work with you.

This activity is great for a variety of options. We've used it to review subject content, assess what young people already know about an upcoming issue we're going to explore, and to establish rules of engagement for how the team will work together.

Set the stage: Starting a new job can reveal assumptions that we make about the organization, what we'll be doing, the rules (which are sometimes unstated), and the people who work or go there. It can happen to everybody.

With the created statements on hand, divide the group into two teams and have them line up behind a marked starting line (tape marks on the floor). Show them the "T" block and the "F" block. Explain that you will read a statement, roll the blocks and the first person in each line should race to grab the block that best represents their opinion. If they think the read statement is true, they should grab the "T" block. If they think it is false, they should attempt to get the "F" block.

Runners return and must explain and defend their answer. The one with the correct answer gains a point for their team. Divulge the answer as well as any necessary clarifying points if needed to further solidify information in their heads.

Make sure you have both blocks back and the next people are in line before reading the next statement.

Ask for any clarifying questions then announce the first statement, roll the blocks, and have the first two participants at the head of each line scramble to get the "right" answer. Continue on, reading as many statements as desired.

Going Deeper
>   » What is the biggest takeaway for you from this activity?
>   » How important is communication in any situation?

- » What assumptions did you realize you hold about __ (fill in the blank: school, work, X club)?
- » Where do those assumptions come from?
- » What strategies can you use to ensure you don't assume?
- » How good are you at asking questions and clarifying expectations?

Field Goals

 10–15 minutes

 butcher paper, painters tape, marker, cones (optional), sticky notes, writing utensils

 Draw a large goal post on a sheet of butcher paper. Tape it to a wall. Mark a line with painters tape (or mark each end with cones) 2–3 feet away.

Make sure everyone in the group has a sticky note and a writing utensil. Explain that their task is to write down a goal they have for themselves or for the group related to the experience. As they think back on all that happened, what do they want to do next? How do they want to use what they learned? Or, where do they want to improve? Give them 2–3 minutes to do individual reflection.

When time is up, instruct everyone to stand up, bring their sticky goals with them, and stand behind the line facing the goal. Taking 4–5 people at a time, instruct the participants to spin gently around 5 times.

Next, ask them to close their eyes and "kick their field goal" by tacking their sticky note between the goal posts. Ask group members who aren't walking at that time to help make sure the field goal kickers don't walk into objects and to encourage them with directions. Make this quick. Do a 5–10 countdown as they wobble over.

Continue with the next group until everyone has gone.

If needed, divide the group into teams and have participants go one at a time, keeping score. One point is awarded each time someone tacks their note between the goal posts. Another option is to use blindfolds and gently spin the field goal kickers yourself before pointing them in the right direction.

Going Deeper
» What kind of goal did you set? Was your goal personal or group based?
» Why is it important to set both personal and group goals?
» Sometimes we achieve our goals on the first try, and sometimes we don't—just like in this game. What should you do if you don't succeed the first time?
» How can we help each other achieve our goals?

NOTES

_____
_____
_____
_____
_____
_____
_____
_____
_____
_____
_____
_____
_____
_____
_____
_____
_____
_____
_____
_____
_____

Bonus!

Seasons of Service: Engaging Youth in Service-Learning Throughout the Year is a free collection of service-learning curriculum lesson plans to engage youth in service-learning and build their leadership skills so they can continue to change their world. Seasons of Service includes 12 interactive lessons on service-learning, three half-day advocacy experiences to celebrate Martin Luther King Day, 11 fully outlined service-learning experiences for young people, and a service-learning journal for young people.

To get your free copy, email us at **team@WriteCreationsGroup. com** or go to **www.writecreationsgroup.com/bonus**.

WE COULDN'T HAVE DONE IT WITHOUT THEM

Working on a book for us is often a community effort because so many wonderful practitioners in the field who are doing incredible work with young people and adults contribute to our efforts.

And we are always happy to lift up that work and honor others. A huge thank you goes to some folks for inspiring ideas or giving us a framework of an activity to play with and adapt: George H. Donigian (Conversation Angles and Service End Angles), author of multiple books, including *Three Prayers You'll Want to Pray* and other titles, Christin Shatzer (1–2–3 Newbie Entrance and 3–2–1 Exit), Associate Director of General Education and the Director of Service-Learning for Lipscomb University's SALT Program, Justin Crowe (Head/Heart/Hands/Feet), Extension Specialist, 4-H Youth Development, University of Tennessee Extension, Derek Peterson (Balloon Keep Up), Child/Youth Advocate and founder of ICAR-US, the Institute for Community & Adolescent Resiliency, Crys Zinkiewicz (OWL), senior editor of youth resources for Abingdon Press (retired) and Dan Horgan (Teaching Myself, Peaks and Valleys, Sticky Note Successes and Challenges, and Zoom In/Zoom Out), Senior Director of Corporate Engagement at MENTOR: The National Mentoring Partnership, youth and leadership development trainer and author of *Tell Me I Can't and I Will*.

We adapted three activities from a couple of our own books: *Groups, Troops, Clubs and Classrooms: The Essential Handbook for Working With Youth* (Sentence Reflection, page 71), *Great Group Games: 175 Boredom-Busting, Zero-Prep Team Builders for All Ages* (Opposite Ends) and *Great Group Games for Kids: 150 Meaningful Activities for Any Setting* (Shuffle, Shuffle).

Other hands make this resource possible including practitioners who read or test ideas and give valuable feedback from their wealth of experience. Our Beta Team includes: Nancy Dickson, Susannah Fotopolous, Karlene Polk, Chip Harris, Melanie Eby, Brian Cooksey, and Terry Silver.

And then there are our editors. Gotta love them! Can't do without them! Writers can go on forever because we have a lot to say. Thanks to Crys Zinkiewicz and Jackie Hansom, this manuscript is sharper.

Finally, if it weren't for a core group of fabulous independent press staff teams, this book wouldn't have happened. These folks coached us all the way through the publishing process. From questions minute to big picture, they helped launch us into publishing. Larry N. Martin started me on the path; John Hartness pointed the way (again and again); Melissa McArthur filled in the gaps; Chris Kennedy set me straight when I was at a crossroads; Jason Graves answered questions.

Susan Roddey did amazing cover and formatting! Love it!

And then there's Jim Nettles, of Authors Essentials, who had no idea he was adopting us for the long haul when he took that phone call and became our coach.

It is a village.

ABOUT THE AUTHORS

Susan Ragsdale and Ann Saylor are nationally-recognized positive youth development specialists and authors with 10 titles to their names, including best-seller *Great Group Games: 175 Boredom-Busting, Zero-Prep Team Builders for All Ages*.

Through Write Creations Group, LLC, they partner with youth-focused agencies to write curriculum and facilitate professional development for youth and youth-serving professionals in leadership, team building, service-learning, program strategies, and youth development best practices. Often called "engaging" and "great presenters," their teaching is grounded in experiential learning, making workshops and curriculum fun while still maintaining depth and meaning.

Both Susan and Ann live in Tennessee.

Connect with Susan Ragsdale & Ann Saylor Online:

- Facebook: @WriteCreationsGroup
- Website: www.WriteCreationsGroup.com
- Instagram: @writecreationsgroup
- Twitter: @Write_Creations
- Newsletter: sign up at www.WriteCreationsGroup.com

Like this book? Please write a review.

Sneak Peek

The following activites are the type of exercises you'll find in *Great Group Leaders*, from Write Creations Group, LLC.

I Do Too!

 5–10 minutes

 statements

Gather the group in a seated circle. Read each statement and ask the group to jump up and point both of their thumbs toward their chests saying, "I do too!" if the statement is true for them. Explain that the intent of this exercise is to get a feel for what people think and their experiences in volunteering and leadership thus far.

Explain that the first statement is a practice round. The statement is: "I like pizza." Restate that anyone who likes pizza should jump up, point their thumbs toward their chest and yell, "I do too!" After a pause, ask those who are standing to sit down.

Do as many statements as desired. Adapt statements as needed for your particular group.

Statements
- I care about people and what happens to them…even those I don't know personally.
- I want to make the world a better place.
- I believe it is important to vote.
- When I see someone being treated wrongly or unfairly, I believe it's important to take some kind of action.
- I have a cause I care about greatly.

- I know young people can impact issues.
- I see myself as a leader.
- I believe that what happens in another country or even another town affects me.
- I am actively involved in volunteering and serving others.
- I have ideas for what we can do to address some community problems.
- I speak up or out for people and issues I care about.
- I have participated or currently participate in march-ins, sit-ins, or in candlelight ceremonies.
- I have written or currently write to political officials or newspapers to express my opinions on pressing issues.
- I have helped or currently help advocate for peers and others to get involved in community issues.
- I have skills and talents I can put to work to better my community.
- I have been in charge of or have started a project or initiative to address a community need.
- I am eager to be involved in making a difference.

Going Deeper

» How did it feel to hear other voices saying, "I do too!" in agreement with you?

» What did you learn about yourself from this activity?

» What is one thing you are proud of about yourself?

» Which statements excite you because there were multiple voices in agreement?

» Which statements stood out to you because there weren't that many voices in agreement but that statement was important to you?

» What other statements would you like declared to see what our group thinks or has experienced with regards to serving and/or leading?

» What is the cause you'd like to hear everyone say, "I do too!" when to comes to solving THAT need in the world?

Your Next Leader

 15–20 minutes

 paper, writing utensils

Divide the group into smaller teams of 3–6. Distribute paper and writing utensils. Ask each team to vertically write the words YOUR NEXT LEADER. For each letter of this acrostic, they should think about a quality, value, skill, or attitude they personally have that can fit each letter. What makes them desirable as a leader? Why should/ would businesses, groups, or organizations want them on their team? Give them 5 minutes to work.

Next, give teams 3 minutes to create a 30-second commercial to promote themselves as Your Next Leaders. When time is up, take turns having teams perform their creation.

Going Deeper

> » What attributes do you think most employers value the most?
> » What quality do you feel is your strongest as a potential employee? What about as a leader? Are the two the same? Why or why not?
> » What strength do you have that you feel is unique to you?
> » How will your particular skill set add to wherever you work or volunteer? What do you bring that will enhance/add/improve any group you're part of?
> » What strengths were particular to us as a group?
> » What qualities are unique to our particular group? How can we leverage our strengths and talents to make a difference in _____(fill in the blank: X project? As a club? Etc.)

Diversity What?

 15–25 minutes

 writing utensils, index cards

 Look up and record the Webster definition of diversity on an index card.

Say: "Diversity means different things to different people. If you asked a 3rd grader what diversity means, you would get a completely different definition than when you ask a 70-year-old. The experience—or lack thereof—of diversity colors everyone's understanding of diversity in a substantial way. Those different filters and experiences can create frustration and miscommunication even when it's caring individuals who are trying to craft a diversity training or experience. To offset that frustration and miscommunication, we want to explore how we all understand diversity."

Divide the group into teams of 3–4. Distribute writing utensils and index cards. Give them 15 minutes to discuss diversity and craft how they would define it. Each team should write their team name (or contributor names) on their definition.

When time is up, collect all the definitions.

Tell them that you are going to read each definition, one at a time, and participants should vote for what they think the real Webster definition of diversity is. Allow 1–2 minutes for teams to discuss after having read all the definitions. After revealing the real definition, applaud definitions that got the most vote and any teams who may have guessed the official definition.

Going Deeper

» How does the "official" definition resonate with you? Does it fit your idea or experience of diversity?

» Is it inclusive? Does it leave anything out? If so, what?

» What was common to our different understandings of diversity?

» What, if anything, surprised you to hear?

» What can we agree on in our understanding of diversity?

» What aspects do we want to honor?

» What aspects do we need to take a hard look and work on to reach understanding and mutual respect?

» What tips can we give others to help them embrace and value diversity?

If you found any of the activities in this book useful, keep reading for information about our other titles.

ALSO BY SUSAN RAGSDALE & ANN SAYLOR

BOOKS FROM SEARCH INSTITUTE

- Great Group Games: 175 Boredom-Busting Zero-Prep Team Builders for All Ages
- Great Group Games for Kids: 150 Meaningful Activities for Any Setting
- Building Character from the Start: 201 Activities to Foster Creativity, Literacy, & Play
- Great Group Games Cards on the Go: 50 Favorite Team Builders
- Get Things Going! 85 Asset-building Activities for Workshops, Presentations, and Meetings
- Groups, Troops, Clubs & Classrooms: The Essential Handbook for Working with Youth

E-BOOKS FROM ABINGDON PRESS

- Ready to Go Service Projects: 140 Ways for Youth Groups to Lend A Hand

GAMES FROM FREE SPIRIT PUBLISHING

- Brain Boosters for Groups in a Jar®
- Imagination Boosters for Groups in a Jar®

E-BOOKS FROM WRITE CREATIONS GROUP, LLC

- Great Group Games Dice Edition: Crazy Challenges, Intriguing Icebreakers, Engaging Energizers

write creations group

Our staff team at Write Creations Group, LLC is known for using research-based strategies to craft fun, interactive and applicable training experiences.

WHAT WE DO

- Develop resources, curriculum and training modules
- Facilitate experiential training and retreat experiences
- Provide workshops or keynotes for conferences

Additionally, we have 891 published strategies and activities to engage groups available at Search Institute Press and Free Spirit. You can peruse and purchase our books at your favorite online bookseller or contact us if you want to order in bulk.

Sample of Topics from our Professional Development Training Tracks:

- A Strength-based Approach to Positive Youth Development
- The Great Group Games Method for Building Relationships and Teams
- Serving from Your Sparks
- Brain Boosters for Groups
- Caring School Climate Retreat
- Engage Youth: Find and Connect with a Sense of Purpose
- Growing Kids Through Literacy, Creativity and Play
- Helping Students Change the World through Service-Learning
- Power is a 2-Way Street
- Leadership Essentials

To find out more about how we can help and hiring our team, contact us at team@WriteCreationsGroup.com.

Jackie Hansom, Ann Saylor & Susan Ragsdale

Write Creations Group, LLC, 615.262.9676, www.WriteCreationsGroup.com, Twitter@Write_Creations, FB: Write Creations Group, LLC

The Art of Facilitating Team Building
The Know-How and Skills to Build Effective Teams through Play!

Sample handout from our full-day training.
Contact us to find out more details about this training.

Learning from the game won't come alive until you take the time to talk about it together.

Debriefing: The Why
Encourages participants to consciously learn through the games, solidifies their understanding, and helps them apply experiences to their everyday life. Reflection is a critical piece!

The Art of Asking Questions and Facilitating Discussion
» Ask open-ended questions that encourage participants to share their insights and feelings
  ◊ Be comfortable with silence. After asking the question, count to 11 Mississippi's slowly before interrupting the silence. This trick allows introverts time to reflect before speaking.
  ◊ Listen to their answers, then go deeper into the conversation.
» Rule of Three:

1. The Game	1. What happened?
2. The Process	2. Why did it happen that way?
3. Real Life	3. How do you relate that to real life?

» Focus on the group process, not just the game's outcome: *Were you successful? Remember, our objectives for today are ___. For me, success relates to these objectives, not whether or not you achieved the game's outcome. It's more about the process than the solution. So...were you successful? Tell me about the process you went through. (We listened to each other. We tried something new.) How could you use those same tools back at your school?*

» Encouraging Reflection:
  ◊ With talkative and self-reflective groups, try having them focus on one main thing that they have learned.
  ◊ For groups that are learning the art of self-expression or introverts, consider physical and artistic reflection activities, such as:
    · Shuffle, Shuffle
    · Thumbs Up/Thumbs Down
    · Whip
    · Puzzle Relay

» See suggested Developmental Asset connections at the end of each game.

» You can play the same games with people ages 10-70 in environments from older elementary students to corporate offices. It's the way that you discuss the games that's different. For example, the Hula Hoop Challenge can focus groups on different learning objectives:
  ◊ 10 year olds: Stay together. Success comes by paying attention to one another and learning from one another.
  ◊ Corporate: Develop a process and stick with it. Once you've done something once, how fast can you do it again?

Spreading Conversation

» A good facilitator won't let one person dominate. Arrange the situation so that no one person is the center of attention.

Why Play: The Developmental Side

A NATURAL PART OF GROWTH

» Play provides the opportunity to connect with others and with meaning and purpose.

» It is engaging and engages the whole person—mind, body, and spirit (creativity, critical thinking, kinetics).

» It involves multiple learning styles through creative, physical, verbal and intellectual stimulation.

» It provides a playground for practicing how to socialize and interact with others.

» Play provides opportunities to explore meaning, apply life lessons and practice new skills and behaviors.

Essential to healthy social, emotional and physical development

» Fosters values clarification

» Demonstrates the value and understanding of positive boundaries

- » Encourages positive risk-taking
- » Promotes mutual respect and understanding
- » Creates a venue for relationship building and bonding
- » Teaches communication skills and how to play well together (cooperation)
- »

Health benefits that continue in life

- » Play refreshes, invigorates, renews and energizes
- » It allows breaks from tensions
- » It provides fresh perspective, allows one to gain clarity and tap into creativity
- » Play evokes laughter (which helps maintain overall health and well-being)

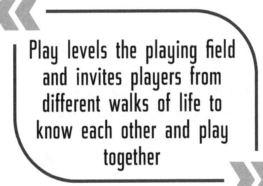

Play levels the playing field and invites players from different walks of life to know each other and play together

Play teaches one to be mindful

- » Of others
- » Of safety—emotional and physical
- » Of self—emotional awareness, values held

Tips for Game Leaders

To make sure game time passes smoothly, tailor every game to your specific group's style and needs. You can easily adapt most games in this book to suit people of varied abilities and skill levels, but you might need to be creative with your resources and space. Consider any limitations as you schedule and plan games. Here are some questions you'll need to consider:

Who's Playing?

Abilities—The physical and mental development of individuals in the group will greatly affect the game's outcome. Consider everyone's potential participation. Are participants:

- Coordinated and strong enough to handle any physical challenges?
- Intellectually able to meet the game's degree of difficulty?
- Old enough to appreciate and learn from the issues the game raises?
- Able to use favorite learning styles with the games you've chosen?

Sensitivities—Games offer the perfect opportunity to explore issues such as diversity, respect, and communication. Consider any particularly touchy issues that might relate to the game before playing. Be prepared to set the game up, lead the activity, and debrief it in a safe way. Are group members:

- Comfortable with the physical interaction required by the game? Mature enough to talk and listen openly to one another without laughing, snickering, and belittling?

- Accepting of playing games in mixed-gender groups? Single-gender groups?

Group Size—Game success can depend on the number of participants. If your group is too large or small for a particular game, could you:
- Split into smaller groups or combine several groups and recruit additional game leaders?
- Adapt the game to fit the group size?

What Materials Do You Need?

Preparation—Before game time, gather, as necessary, any of the following:

- Props (e.g., tennis balls, soft fabric balls, chart paper and markers, stopwatch, bandannas, string, masking tape, nametags)
- Paper and pens for note-taking
- Coaches, judges, supporters, demonstrators

When Are You Playing?

Time Parameters—Suggested time ranges are provided for each game in this book. The time your group may require can depend on several factors, including who's in the group, how many, and how much time you have. Make sure to include enough time for playing the game, as well as for asking reflection questions. Ask yourself:

- How much time can we take to play a game?
- Is the game quick to learn, or does it take more explaining and practicing?

Energy Level—Games in this book range from calm and quiet to loud and active. Think through your agenda and what you'll be doing. Do you need to:

- Boost energy in the middle of a meeting or class?
- Focus your group's attention?
- Fill the whole day?

Where Are You Playing?

Indoors or Outdoors—You can play most of the games in this book indoors or outdoors, but keep in mind weather conditions that might affect plans. Be sure to locate available bathrooms. If it's hot outside, don't forget to bring water bottles. Consider the following:

- Is the area large enough for the group?
- Are tree roots or holes in the way? Are structural columns or furniture blocking the space? Are exposed nails or other hazards to be avoided?
- Will your group's noise disturb others? Is the space quiet enough for participants to focus?
- Are the acoustics good?

Why Are You Playing?

Goals—Always identify the goals of your game and keep them in mind as you play. Use your goals as a framework for instructing, facilitating, and debriefing. Ask yourself:

- Do you want to play a game to set the tone for a meeting or class or for some other occasion?
- What do you want your group to achieve by the end of the game?

While the book is designed to help organizations and schools embrace a strength-based approach to working with youth through the Developmental Assets, these same activities can be used in businesses and nonprofits by just shifting the direction of the conversation slightly.

30 Second Spotlight

Purpose: To provide a platform for participants to get to know each other on a more personal level as well as sharing what they believe is important.

Estimated Time: 5 minutes or less

Supplies: timer

Give a topic for groups to talk about in their table groups. Tell them that each person will have 30 seconds of uninterrupted time to talk about the given topic. Tell table groups that the person who had to drive the farthest from the current location will be the first speaker. Give a signal for the first speakers to start speaking. When time is up, signal the speakers to quit talking and for the next speakers to begin. Continue, keeping time until everyone has had a chance to speak.

Possible topics: cooking, vacations, family, the weekend, hobby, best day ever, place of worship, most prized possession, best book/movie ever

Wrap Up:

Taking 30 seconds to share from the hip and listen to each other may not seem like much, but making the effort to connect with each other in small ways adds up for more powerful relationships as we pull in all of who we are. Listening and learning about each other leads to respect, understanding and trust – key elements in working together successfully and as a team.

Key Elements:

Communication, Celebration, Community Building, Team Building

TIP

This activity pushes each person to share on the spot, which can be challenging for some, skill building and informative. Topics can be easy to allow for comfort and ease in practicing communication skills or they can be inspiration and insightful, such as when participants share about particular assets and why they value them. Choose topics based on where your group is and what you need to accomplish: build relationships, encourage light-hearted fun or delve more deeply into the assets and the work your group is doing.

Quick Thinking

Purpose: To promote positive relationships and activities for young people.

Estimated Time: 15 minutes

Supplies: index cards, pens

Preparation: Make Alphabet Cards by writing one alphabet letter on each index card (or buy alphabet flash cards). Make Thought-prompter Cards by writing these teasers on index cards:

» Books that every young person should read
» Influential people
» Recreational activities for young people
» Musical instruments
» Things associated with a playground
» Things associated with the kitchen
» Musical group/vocal or instrumental
» Things associated with volunteering
» Places to volunteer
» Ways to make a difference
» Ways to use skills and talents
» Important values
» Family traditions
» Something to be proud of or something that makes me proud
» Ways to help others
» Ways to show others that you care
» Movies every young people should watch
» Somewhere every young person should go/visit
» Favorite way to spend time
» Something every young person should know how to do

Divide the group into teams of 5-7 people. Each team should send a representative to the game table for the first round. Have one person draw an alphabet card and a prompter card and flip them both over. The team representatives should quickly think of something that connects the alphabet letter and the category together. For example the letter "S" and "books every young person should read" might yield the response, "Sherlock Holmes." When they think of an answer, they should raise their hand to give their answer. The first team to give a viable match wins a point. Teams then send up new representatives for the next round. Continue rotations until time is called. The team with the most points wins the game.

Wrap Up:
This activity is a fun way to think about ways to promote positive relationships, self-image and involvement.
- » What other cards would you create to learn more about others?
- » What are the things in your life that help you be strong?
- » What are ways that you help others be strong of character and values?

Key Elements:
Communication, Working Together, Vision

Geometric Reflection

Purpose:	To close the meeting with a reflection on what participants learned.
Estimated Time:	5–10 minutes
Supplies:	pre-designed chart paper
Preparation:	Draw the following shapes down the left-hand side of the chart paper: bubbles used with cartoon characters (when they're speaking), a circle, a square and a cloud like drawing.

Ask participants to use one of the drawings to prompt their responses in small groups of 4 (if the training/meeting is bigger than 12 people).

- » Something that is bubbling up within me ... (cartoon character bubbles)
- » Something that keeps going round in my head ... (circle)
- » These two things square with my belief ... (square)
- » I've been wondering about ... (cloud)

Key Elements:
Vision, Celebration, Working Together, Communication

Growing up can be difficult. Will I be picked last? Will I make the team? Do people like me? How do I fit in? Wait! What I really want is to belong. The swirling tide of emotions and challenges leave many feeling insecure, uncertain and at times, like a loser.

What if a roll of the dice could change that? he games are designed with an eye on the skills everyone needs to navigate life like a champ: relationship skills, team work, overcoming challenges. They also focus on creativity, which works in tandem with problem-solving..

Anyone Want to Play?

Of course you do! Who doesn't like to play? Ann Saylor and I (Susan Ragsdale) have discovered the power of play: It makes program and classroom time so much more fun, and it makes learning "stick." In our 20+ years of working with both youth and their adult leaders, we've used games and activities as the backbone of our books and as our main educational strategy in our workshops.

Truth be told, we realized play's value when we were school-age children ourselves as we were babysitting, teaching swimming lessons, tutoring, and leading activities at church and overnight camps. Even then, we recognized the importance of play for people of all ages.

Consequently, Ann and I focus on the benefits of play in our work. We love creating spaces for laughter, relationship-building, stress-relief and improved well-being to take place. Play can create moments in which to realize mini-life lessons. Play makes space for people to be themselves. It is a platform for discovery because it spans cultures, ages and differences. As such, it allows and encourages friendships to bud and take root. Play can also help change the group environment to calming or to energizing, depending on what is needed.

Best of all, in the midst of having fun, play is purposeful. It boosts brainpower with its various elements of movement, novelty, music, challenge, humor, and deep conversations that arise with many games. Specifically, play creates opportunities for them to explore their interests, and it sets the stage for them to identify what is meaningful to them. It provides moments for individuals to be in charge, further developing useful leadership skills, communication skills, and self-confidence.

Play With Purpose

We know these games will get groups moving, laughing, sharing and competing. When Ann and I work with youth and adults, enjoying the experience and having fun are two of our foundational tenets. Growing up is hard and often full of stress, so creating those moments of whimsy is important. Lighten it up!

Another intentional strategy in our work is "movement." Young people sit in classes for hours on end. They often need to move to recharge, energize and get their mojo back...and maybe even their happy face.

These are the givens—play and move, enjoy and laugh! However, while playing these games and having a good time, your group is also engaged in "play with purpose." That purpose element invites discovery. That discovery might be about an aha within the group or involve a life lesson. The aspects participants explore will serve them well in their lives. The dice games will help youth grow in attitude, character, sense of self, awareness and people skills. In both playing the games and talking about their experiences, youth will develop in these key areas:

» **Relationship skills.** Whether the roll of the die prompts players to share facts about themselves, or challenges them to find commonalities with a partner, or jump starts a conversation, these games provide the opportunity for youth to connect and practice forming positive relationships. Additionally, youth further practice verbal and nonverbal communication.

» **Teamwork.** Research shows that people are hardwired to connect with others. They want meaningful social interactions. Working together in teams is a necessary learning for sports, classroom work, and careers. Cooperation is key. Learning how to work together is so much more fun when done through games, learning how to play together.

» **Challenge.** Sometimes masked as competition, facing challenges offers participants opportunities to take risks and work on skills such as problem-solving, critical thinking, being flexible and self-regulating one's emotions. "Losing" a challenge can also help individuals and teams learn from the setbacks: What worked? What didn't work? What might I/we do differently next time? Did I do my best? What is my own attitude when I'm not number one? How am I responding? And, what might I need to work further on to be the best me I can be?

» **Creativity.** Dance. Music. Paintings. Photography. Decorating cookies. Woodworking... Being creative is a natural expression of selfhood. Whether it is sparked by novelty or sparks novelty, creativity opens up possibilities for expression and boosts brainpower. Creativity is also the primary ally for innovation and real world problem solving. Creative thinking is the skill of getting out of the box. When tapped, creative thinking moves us beyond linear thinking to more synergistic approaches; making new connections or associations between stimuli. As a result, creativity can help develop empathy as people look at situations from different points of view. The ability to consider varying perspectives further cements strong relationships with others. Finally, creativity is a outlet for stress relief and self-management of emotions—a perfect tool for everyone's toolkit!

Beyond these four focus areas, the questions found at the end of each game in the Going Deeper section delve into reflection and conversations that reinforce positive values, sense of self, social-emotional learning, decision making and leadership. Thinking through and discussing the ideas and experiences that arise in the games and in those conversations are often catalysts for participants to grow emotionally and socially as well as in the four other key areas noted.

It's Not a Number, It's a...

Prep: Gather paper and writing utensils.

Divide the group into pairs and distribute paper and pencils. Explain that each pair should roll a die and write the number they roll onto a piece of paper. Give pairs 2 minutes to make a SIMPLE sketch that somehow includes part of their number. For example, a 6 might become the wing of a butterfly or part of a pair of glasses or a 1 might become the stem of a flower or the side of a building.

Do a simple example together as a group, asking them all for ideas on how to turn the number into a portion of a picture. Demonstrate how, once they write the number down, they can turn the page around and look at the number from different angles to get new ideas. Let pairs play. Share drawings when done. Have the group vote by applause for the most creative, the most lifelike, the funniest, the most artistic... Instruct them to applaud for everyone, but to clap the loudest for the creation in each category that they like best.

Variation

If you have a large group, the game leader can roll the die and randomly assign numbers to different pairs. Or, have multiple dice and let players quickly pass the die from pair to pair.

This game pairs well with the children's stories Not a Box *and* Not a Stick *by Antoinette Portis, as well as* The Turn-Around Upside-Down Alphabet Book *by Lisa Campbell Ernst. You might choose to read the story first, then play the game to help enhance comprehension of imagination and perspective.*

Going Deeper

We looked for how we could create something new or different from a starting figure. That activity required tapping into our imaginations and looking at things from different angles. Sometimes when we get into disagreements, it's really helpful to look at things from the other person's eyes (a different angle). Where else might you benefit from looking at things from different angles? (Possible answers: Meeting people from different cultures, resolving conflicts, problem-solving and so on.)

Key Elements

Creativity

Dicey Conversations

Have the group sit down in a circle. Have someone roll the die. He chooses someone else from the group to answer the question that corresponds to the number rolled. After the player answers the question, she rolls the die and picks the next person to answer the new question corresponding with the number rolled. It's okay if the same die number is rolled as the time before.

Continue rolling and asking different players questions until all 6 questions have been asked and answered, or until everyone has had the opportunity to have a turn.
   » What are outdoor activities you like to do on a sunny day?
   » What is your favorite animal and why?
   » How do you like to spend time with your family?
   » What is your favorite homemade food? Why?
   » Who is a famous person you'd like to meet and why?
   » What is one pet you would like to have and why?

   If your group is larger than 8-10 players, you might want to have multiple circles and give each group a set of the questions for reference.

Going Deeper
What is a fun question you'd like to have everyone in the group answer? Let some ask their questions and take turns answering them.

Key Elements
Relationship Skills

Stack-up Cup Relay: The Team Approach

Prep: Place 6 cups of the same size (plastic or paper) with a die atop a level surface of some kind (table, floor, etc.) 15–20' away from each team.

Divide the group into even teams of 4-6 players. Have teams line up, relay-style, behind the starting line.

The goal is for each team to quickly stack their set of cups up pyramid style, with 3 cups on the bottom, 2 on the middle layer and 1 on top. The first player in each team runs to his team's stack of cups. He will first roll the die as many times as needed until he rolls a 1 or a 6. Once he rolls one of those numbers, he places only ONE cup for his team's pyramid. Once he's placed his cup, he runs back and tags the next player in line. That player rolls the die until she can place her cup on the pyramid. Players continue this process—roll, get a 1 or 6, add a cup and tag the next person in line—until the last person has added the last cup. That player then collapses down all the cups to a single stack and races back to her team. The first team to complete their group pyramid wins.

Variation
To speed up the process, let players build every time an even number is rolled.

Going Deeper

To achieve the goal took a little bit of luck, teamwork and a lot of patience, because the finished task probably didn't come quickly. Where do you have to practice patience in real life? What are you learning or working on that's not coming as quickly as you'd like (but you're keeping at it and trying to get it)?

Key Elements

Teamwork, Challenge

The following activities are reprinted from **Great Group Games on the Go: 50 Favorite Team Builders** by Susan Ragsdale & Ann Saylor with permission. © 2012 Search Institute Press, Minneapolis, Minnesota; 800-888-7828; www.search-institute.org. All rights reserved.

Names in Action

Time: 10-30 minutes

The Game

Ask players to introduce themselves to the group, one by one, by pairing each syllable of their name with a fun motion as they say their name out loud. (For example, Crystal has two syllables in her name, so she puts her hands on her hips when she says *Crys* and bobs her head with *tal*.) The group members respond to each person by repeating the name with the same action to affirm the person and learn the name for themselves. As each new person introduces him—or herself, ask the group to repeat the new name and then start from the top repeating each previous person's name and action.

Variation:

(For the brave, bold, and those who want to have fun!) After all youth have introduced themselves to the group, play a dance music compilation and call out names of group members at random. Everyone dances to the motions of each name as you call it out.

Asset Categories:

Support, Empowerment, Constructive Use of Time, Social Competencies

Stage One Group Development:

Starting Off Right

Last Detail

Time: 5–10 minutes

The Game

Ask players to find a partner and stand back-to-back. Tell them to change three things about themselves without saying anything (for example, take off your glasses, switch your hair part, or roll up your sleeve). On cue, partners turn around to face each other and try to guess what was changed. Pairs can do this a couple times, each time leaving previous changes in place.

Going Deeper:
- » In what ways do you think change can be positive or negative? Easy or difficult?
- » In what ways does your behavior change, depending upon whether you're with your family or your friends and teammates?
- » How might this group change over time?
- » What changes might you make to work most effectively together?
- » How can you be caring and respectful of others even when you disagree with them?
- » What systems allow you to give adults feedback on what's working and what you'd like to change in your school or organization?
- » How can you use the power of your beliefs to make your school community better?

» Change can be uncomfortable. What are ways you can help others accept changes that must occur? How can you contribute to the change you want to see?

» What action can you take each day to make others feel accepted?

Asset Categories:
Empowerment, Social Competencies, Support, Boundaries and Expectations, Positive Identity

Stage Four Group Development:
Deepening Trust

Predators and Prey in the City

Time: 20–30 minutes

Supplies: One blindfold

The Game

Designate one person the "prey" and have that person sit in the middle of the playing area with a blindfold securely tied over his or her eyes—no peeking! Tell remaining players ("predators") to position themselves randomly around the prey, at least 10 to 15 feet away. When you give the signal, predators try as quietly as possible to sneak up on the prey. Their goal is to be the one predator who tags the prey without being caught. The prey's goal is to stop the predators by using a keen sense of hearing to detect movements and point at them to "freeze" predators in their tracks. Once frozen, predators can no longer move or make any sounds. The game ends when either a predator tags the prey or the prey freezes all predators. If a predator successfully tags the prey, she or he becomes the new prey.

Going Deeper:

> » How did it feel to be the prey?
> » How can listening save you from "getting into trouble" or mishearing what others say?
> » What strategies did you use as predators to tag the prey?
> » What things may prey on you? How can you protect yourself from danger?
> » What influences in your life can help insulate you from harm? Friends? Caring adults? Personal commitments? Attitudes? Values? Skills?

» What can you do to sharpen your own "senses" in order to protect yourself from harm?

» How can you help protect others?

Asset Categories:
Social Competencies, Positive Identity, Positive Values, Commitment to Learning, Support, Empowerment

Stage Three Group Development:
Becoming a Team

Groups, Troops, Clubs & Classrooms: The Essential Handbook For Working With Youth

Excerpt from Chapter 1:
A Strength-Based Approach to Positive Youth Development

Building on Strengths Is Counter-Cultural

Derek Peterson, an international youth advocate, wrote the following advice about working with young people:

NO...person should use the label "at risk." It is meaningless. It is quackery. It drives the mind and the community to ridiculous actions, that, too often, further harm kids. I know that we all live in a deficit based culture, and are paid to identify and fix problems, repair broken teens, and make dysfunctional families and communities work. However, what asset based thinking brings to the conversation is that 1) everybody has things that are RIGHT about them, 2) we can fix a problem by

approaching the solution through our strengths and competencies, 3) we can't repair a broken teen, but we can show him/
her her resilience, and have them understand that we have all
been broken at one time or another, and we'll probably become
broken again—life is difficult, and 4) we can't make anyone do
anything. All we can do is enter their circle, support others in
seeing the world through different eyes, provide the tools and
knowledge to move toward their identified goal and way of being, and then work alongside them to make it all happen . . .
CELEBRATING and LAUGHING all the way, while constantly
rewarding RELATIVE BEST."

The act of focusing on strengths is different from the cultural norm
of zoning in on what needs "fixing." The danger of a "fixing" mentality
is that you can unknowingly create a gap between you and those you
love. The tendency is to see youth as lesser than yourself.

A strength-based approach calls for seeing youth as whole and in
light of their capabilities, strengths, and possibilities. So instead of
approaching youth with the idea that you are going to fix them somehow, look closely for their strengths. Instead of focusing on "what's
wrong" with a child, look within him or her to find talents, gifts, and
inner resources to draw out. You start with what is right, good, and
strong within and about them and use those innate gifts to foster positive growth. You emphasize the positive.

Here is another insight from Derek Peterson on how to approach
young people:

"I have found that, for the most part, I live in to the stories that
people tell me about. If those who have influence upon me believed
in me, and communicated those positive expectations, and gave me
opportunities to practice and grow into those expectations, and finally
celebrated my "relative best" attempts, then, for the most part I lived
into those expectations."

We believe in the best of youth. Always. And that belief shows up and plays out in what we say and do on a consistent basis. And we work from strengths rather than from deficits. We work to help youth realize their potential and to gain a healthy sense of self. We work to set expectations of them and of ourselves to live into our own innate goodness.

Positive youth development is steeped in a belief that youth have value now, not just when they become adults. Youth have important things to say about culture, education, and decisions. They have unique perspectives and can contribute to solving today's problems, so it's important to strive to engage them in the conversation. Your role is to provide opportunities for youth to give back, work side-by-side with others, and have roles that are meaningful and impactful. You offer supportive relationships and guidance.

Excerpt from Chapter 7: Know Them

Know Their Culture and Background

Part of knowing your youth is knowing where they come from—their cultural backgrounds as well as the distinct nature of youth culture and norms. Youth identify themselves in many ways. They may define themselves by dress, interests, music, economic class, ethnicity, physical challenges, learning differences or learning styles, sexual identity, being technologically bilingual, and so many more aspects that make each of us unique and different.

Even with these differences, you and your group must recognize that every child is valuable and has innate gifts. When someone is labeled "different"—be that from identity, ethnicity, abilities or even personality quirks—the space we create within our group needs to be strong and supportive and free of prejudices, offering hospitality, acceptance, and appreciation for each young person.

Initial Thoughts

Do I have any stumbling blocks in working with various youth? Do I have a place of discomfort or prejudice that I need to examine that may get in the way of me offering acceptance and love?

Why is it important for me to understand youth culture and the various ways youth self-identify?

How Culturally Savvy are You about Your Group?

Quiz yourself to see how up you are on your young people's heritage and youth culture. Read through each set of subquestions and highlight the three that are most meaningful to you.

How well do you . . . know them?
- Do you know what name they want to go by—their given name or a nickname?
- Do you know how to pronounce it correctly?
- Do you know their skills and interests?
- Do you know whether they have food allergies? Are any sick with a critical illness? Are any on medications?
- Do you know whether they have experienced a personal trauma?
- Do you know whether they have a learning difference?
- Do you know their Multiple Intelligences bent?

How well do you . . . know their world?
- Do you know what their primary, first language is?
- Do you know the current trends in youth dress?
- Do you know the cultural requirements of their dress (dresses, covering faces . . .)?

- Do you know their rituals and traditions?
- What's the popular manner for greeting each other? Knuckle bump? Something else?
- Do you know their music? What are the top five songs/bands/ groups your group is listening to?
- Do you know the social media venues they use to keep up with each other?
- Do you keep up with the books, movies, and art interests that appeal to your age group?

How well do you . . . know their family life?
- Have you met their parents?
- Do you know what the family rules are—the ones that might impact rules you set in your program or classroom?
- Have you asked about their family traditions?
- Do you know whether the family is going through something serious such as a divorce, loss of a loved one, or other major trauma?

How well do you . . . know their spiritual and cultural practices?
- Do you know whether they must pray at a certain time each day?
- Do you know whether they must avoid certain foods?
- Do you know whether they are allowed to touch (shake hands, do a high five) a member of the opposite sex?
- Do you know how they approach holidays? (What holidays do they celebrate? Are any holidays taboo?)
- Do they have meaningful holidays that you should know about?

Sometimes religious or cultural practices might impact what you do or how you do your program. Once you learn them, you can be flexible and adjust your rules so that your rules don't stifle their cultural identities.

Five Keys to Being Culturally Sensitive

Following are some important guidelines to help you be culturally sensitive with you youth:

#1: Always remember that kids are kids. No matter what their heritage, background, self-identification, or what is going on in their lives, kids are kids. When you remember that, the "difference" that you're dealing with fades to the background and you will focus on what's really important about a young person. Chad Harrington, a youth worker with Nations Ministry Center reminds us, "The refugee middle schoolers with whom I work are just like other American students. The biggest difference is that their struggles are simply magnified: social ostracism, academics, and hormones—all present challenges—just more so because of all the cultural differences."

#2: Protect the uniqueness of each young person. Don't let misconceptions breed rampant and destroy your group. Stay educated, educate, and maintain the norm of respect. Create opportunities for youth to learn and grow together so they can experience "difference" and see that "different" isn't that different. Consultant Kelli Walker-Jones advocates that we "stay curious enough not to label them. The point is to see them as a kid, love them, and help them grow. If you don't know something about them, whether it is Tourette's syndrome, their cultural traditions, or what it means to be lesbian, gay, or transgendered, then find out. Get curious and educate yourself for the sake of understanding them personally and being able to offer them support."

#3: Help youth find what they have in common. Discovering commonalities covers a lot of ground in bridging gaps created intergenerationally or even culturally, and it creates a solid base to explore differences and how each person is unique. Anything can be

bridged once you establish how youth are alike. And, no surprise, our number one strategy in finding common ground is by using games as the platform to facilitate that discovery.

#4: Remember that you are the role model. Set a norm for respecting one another, even if you don't understand or fully agree with some of the views. If you have a moment where you feel uncomfortable about a viewpoint, action, or self-identification, stop and do a self-check. Is your reaction from a prejudice? Is it from a lack of knowledge, experience, or understanding? Get yourself a check-in first and then be the model for creating a supportive, loving environment where everyone is valued and accepted.

#5: Be deliberate in finding ways to highlight cultural and self-identification differences as assets to the group. Make sure every unique characteristic has a way to rise up as an asset to the group. Invite youth to share their views, traditions, and culture related to any given topic: cooking, music, art, stories, games, dance, and holiday or religious traditions. Find ways to let your youth lead workshops or teach others about what they know or can do. They can share things such as what it's like to be Muslim, what it's like to grow up in Indonesia, what it's like to have MS, or what it's like to speak two languages. Everyone has something to bring and offer to the group to make it stronger. When you tap into the strengths of who they are, their experiences, and what they're good at doing, you create the space for them to share power and build understanding.

OTHER RAGSDALE & SAYLOR BOOKS

Building on the popularity of the bestselling *Great Group Games*, this new collection for the younger set shows teachers and group leaders how to make even the silliest activity meaningful. Complete with details on timing, supplies, set up, and suggested group size, this is the perfect grab-and-go resource for anyone working with elementary school age children. Far from frivolous, each "play with purpose" game concludes with discussion questions to build positive identity, friendship skills, and a host of other character traits kids need to succeed. (**Search Institute**)

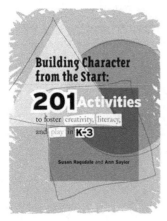

BUILDING CHARACTER FROM THE START: 201 Activities to Foster Creativity, Literacy, & Play

This K–3 activity book helps parents, teachers and youth workers build character through creative activities such as finish the picture coloring pages, picture books that connect to explorative activities, and group games. (**Search Institute**)

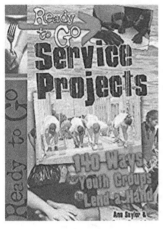

This ready-to-go tool will help youth groups find meaningful ways to connect and make a difference in their communities through service-learning. Practical and interactive activities will help youth consider the connection between faith and service, discover the ways they are uniquely designed to serve, and explore service project ideas. It also profiles activities and conversation starters to help you tap into the power of service-learning for building character, challenging perceptions, and shaping leaders. It's easy for a youth leader to scan and it's flexible enough to use with diverse groups from middle school to college. (**Abingdon Press**)

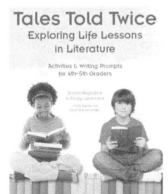

Email us at **team@WriteCreationsGroup. com** or visit **www.writecreationsgroup.com/ bonus** to get a free copy of **Tales Told Twice**, a helpful tool to bring the stories to life and draw out character and life lessons. Fun, engaging activities and writing prompts included for each book.

CPSIA information can be obtained
at www.ICGtesting.com
Printed in the USA
BVHW091318290819
557143BV00017B/2520/P